MAKE IT HAPPEN BLUEPRINT

Praise for

MAKE IT HAPPEN BLUEPRINT

"I do love this book. McCullough is real and relate-able. I was only in the first chapter when I felt hopeful and empowered. While some of her golden advice is aimed mostly to those working in the field of Business (which I am not), there is more than enough real-life help that a Homemaker can use too. She doesn't create yet another list of things "I should be doing," but attainable solutions to MAKE TIME for the other things I really DO need to do. These recommendations are easy to do. I am so thankful for McCullough's inspiration and passion to share this knowledge; my life was immediately changed and improved for the goals her book motivated."

—**Kristin Call**; London, England

"I used to be SO good about planning and doing, but over the past few years, I have become unfocused and thus, unproductive. As a mom of three and an entrepreneur, my two biggest time traps have been multi-tasking and compulsively checking email + social media. Michelle's productivity action tips have been a powerful refresher course for me! I love how she simplifies things with steps that set you up for foolproof success."

—**Heather Allard**, founder heatherallard.com; Rhode Island, USA

"Michelle McCullough has one of those minds you love to be around! She shares fresh ideas, content, and strategies for creating a life and a business that you love. Reading this book will elevate your life!"

—**Tiffany Peterson**, Professional Speaker, www.TiffanySpeaks.com; Utah, USA

"As entrepreneurs we often feel alone. McCullough's book Make It Happen reminds us that we are all in this together. She manages to rekindle your purpose as well as provide pertinent ideas and strategies to help you perform at your best. I love the way she provides a section at the end of each chapter to help you implement the things you read and learn in Make It Happen. Every purposeful entrepreneur should have this book on their nightstand!"

—**Nicole Carpenter**, CEO of MOMentity.com and bestselling author of *52 Weeks to Fortify Your Family: 5-minute messages*; Utah USA

"Michelle's chapter "Raising High Performers" is great! I especially loved the story about her family theme and her son remembering it as he hopped out of the car on the first day of school. Michelle's suggestions and principles really resonated with me and I believe they would absolutely help parents to raise children who thrive!"

—**Tara Kennedy-Kline**, Author of *Stop Raising Einstein*; Pennsylvania, USA

"The beauty of Michelle's book & writing is that it is a lucid, unadorned reminder that we periodically need. It reinforces powerful practices which we often brush past and only remember when we fail to "make it happen." I love her earnest voice and really personal examples."

—**Vilasi Venkatachalam**; India

Praise for

MICHELLE McCULLOUGH

Michelle speaks all across the country at seminars on motivation and marketing. Here is what some of her attendees have to say about Michelle's presentations.

"I loved Michelle's energy and humor. Her content was simple and easy to implement and she kept the audience fully engaged!"

—**Marissa Hyatt**, Tennessee

"Michelle is engaging, insightful and full of epic content. I've learned more from her in a few minutes than I have in some 3-day seminars. Thank You!"

—**Debbie Burns**, Utah

"The energy was incredible. When she finished I felt like it is achievable."

—**Bridgett Peterson**, Nevada

"Great content and tips! Michelle is so excited to share and help you move forward!"

—**Lynn Navares**, Washington

"Great practical content and strategies. Thank you!"

—**Esther Vermillion**, Texas

"I loved her fun personality and amazing depth and breadth of knowledge."

—**Kalyn Robison**, Utah

"She is clear and passionate. Two things I love!"

—**Jen Fanning**

"I loved her enthusiasm knowledge, and spunky sass."

—**Josie Platts**, Utah

"Humor! Thank for adding value AND fun to our afternoon."

—**Stephanie Giesbrecht**, Texas

"Michelle is on top of the latest trends and gives great how-to tips—Thank you!"

—**Tara Reed**, Oregon

"Michelle didn't hold back on information. I couldn't write fast enough. The information was so good. I can't wait for more."

—**Julie Hinton**, Utah

"Michelle provides so much expertise and presents it in such a fun way! I'm so excited to put some new things into practice."

—**Lisa Nelson**, Utah

"The vast knowledge of multiple subjects was astounding. I could listen to her talk about social media strategy all day."

—**Nigel Smith**, California

"I was introduced to ideas that I hadn't considered before, and mediums that I hadn't known much about but that I now see value in. Loved all the simple, doable tips!"

—**Cynthia Patience**, Arizona

"She is a fireball with amazing energy and information."

—**Teisha Hinton**, Utah

"It was packed with action items! I love her energy! We should be B.F.F.'s!"

—**Emily Lesher**, Utah

"Content! Content! Content! I love the rich information Michelle provides. Great value for the time spent!"

—**Hayley Anderson**, Utah

"Her sense of humor, clarity and expertise. Michelle is full of million dollar tips!"

—**Aisha Harley**, Oregon

"She is inspirational and knows her strategy."

—**Teresa Gray**, Washington

"Truck load of valuable tips, I have to go home and break down my notes more, I am sure I will discover even more value."

—**Blake Driggs**, Utah

"Best guest speaker at the entire Elevation event. Hands down."

—**Eve Colantoni**, Florida

"I loved how you simplified something so overwhelming. Thank you."

—**Leslie Phillips**, Idaho

"Michelle's presentation was succinct. Jam packed with useful tips that can be implemented without getting overwhelmed."

—**Andrea Crisp**, Oregon

"Michelle is an enthusiastic and high energy speaker. She is an expert at implementing."

—**John Stoker**, Utah

"Michelle's wit and delivery is amazing. I was laughing so hard while taking crazy notes. I am so excited to get home and implement."

—**Amee Gleave**, Utah

MAKE IT HAPPEN BLUEPRINT

18 HIGH-PERFORMANCE PRACTICES TO CRUSH IT IN LIFE AND BUSINESS WITHOUT BURNING OUT

MICHELLE McCULLOUGH

NEW YORK

NASHVILLE • MELBOURNE • VANCOUVER

MAKE IT HAPPEN BLUEPRINT
18 HIGH-PERFORMANCE PRACTICES TO CRUSH IT IN LIFE AND BUSINESS WITHOUT BURNING OUT

Published in New York, New York, by Morgan James Publishing. Morgan James is a trademark of Morgan James, LLC. www.MorganJamesPublishing.com

The Morgan James Speakers Group can bring authors to your live event. For more information or to book an event visit The Morgan James Speakers Group at www.TheMorganJamesSpeakersGroup.com.

ISBN 978-1-68350-113-8 paperback
ISBN 978-1-68350-115-2 eBook
ISBN 978-1-68350-114-5 hardcover
Library of Congress Control Number: 2016909036

Cover Design by:
Rachel Lopez
www.r2cdesign.com

Interior Design by:
Bonnie Bushman
The Whole Caboodle Graphic Design

In an effort to support local communities, raise awareness and funds, Morgan James Publishing donates a percentage of all book sales for the life of each book to Habitat for Humanity Peninsula and Greater Williamsburg.

Get involved today! Visit
www.MorganJamesBuilds.com

To my kids.
May you always know that you can accomplish anything you want. Nothing brings me greater joy than watching you "Make It Happen"! I'll be on the front row cheering you on.

CONTENTS

FOREWORD

You never hear anybody say, "At the end of the day, I hope I fail." Yet failure seems to be woven into the realities of our everyday lives. With no glamour and plenty of shame associated with it, we don't often have discussions about defeat, what doesn't work, or the times we got it wrong. Why are we so afraid of failure?

The lack of discussion surrounding failure can make it seem as though we're the only ones who can't get things to fall into place. While others carry on with their charmed lives and find success around every turn, we're left slogging away in the trenches, wondering when it will be our time to shine.

To add fuel to the fire, we champion the overnight success stories—the bands that appear out of nowhere and suddenly have chart-topping albums, sold out concerts, and adoring fans on every corner, reality shows that catapult ordinary people to instant stardom (or at least their 15 minutes of fame), launch businesses, and make dreams realities.

This constant parade of achievement can make success seem even more elusive. Either you have the Midas touch, or you don't.

In *Make It Happen Blueprint*, Michelle McCullough lifts the curtain on success to show there is no secret genetic code for high performers, and in fact, everyone has what it takes to be successful. Every so-called "instant success" story comes with a prequel consisting of hard work, heartache, and even failure. Most likely, lots of failure.

As Michelle shares her own stories of triumphs and trials, it becomes clear that success is as much about practice as anything. Success can, in fact, be learned, and it often takes effort to get it right. As Michelle outlines the patterns of high performers, you can feel a sense of excitement building as you come to realize success is within your reach. Successful people are just like you, me, and everybody else. They have wins and losses, but at the end of the day they've learned the habits and skills to keep moving, minimize failures, and ultimately set themselves up to reach their goals.

While Michelle McCullough has a reputation for success, I appreciate her candidness in sharing the stories of times she fell short, the lessons she's learned from failure, and the path she's taken to get where she is today. She draws from her own experiences, and includes the best of what she's learned from years of studying the patterns of high achievers. She artfully incorporates all of this into a book that is real, and provides easy-to-follow guideposts that make it possible for anyone to tread the pathway to success and make things happen in their own lives.

Michelle has a true desire and unique ability to impact individuals, communities and all with whom she comes in contact. She is a sharp, warm, proactive go-getter and knows how to influence the hearts and minds of others for good. Truly, Michelle is a high performer—an authentic leader and role model. As a result, she has an unusual talent for turning challenges into solutions that can yield incredible results. If you were to speak with those associated with Michelle you'd find that her vision catches the imagination of all she associates with. She creates environments of high trust, high goals, and high support. Fortunately, she's packed all this goodness into one book, and now you can take your life and business to the next level just by reading and applying the principles she teaches.

Enjoy and make waves!

Deep respect,
Richie Norton, #1 Bestselling author of
The Power of Starting Something Stupid

INTRODUCTION
THE PRINCIPLE OF PRACTICE

When most kids my age were including a Sony Walkman, LA Gear high tops, and Girbaud Jeans on their Christmas lists, I was dreaming of a Franklin Day Planner. I may be the only 12-year-old in history who was elated to find a "box of success" under the tree, but I spent that holiday break happily writing a mission statement, prioritizing to-do lists, and getting organized.

Planning, productivity, and personal development have always been part of who I was. The Franklin Day Planner was just the beginning.

When I was fourteen, Elaine Millet was my youth group leader. She was caring and kind, and she came into my life at a critical age. She helped me cement my confidence, persistence, and faith.

Elaine always asked me about school and my current ventures. She patted my back and encouraged me in all of my plays, projects, and debate tournaments. Even when it wasn't her job to care anymore, she always took time out of her busy schedule (and with nine children of her own, you can imagine how busy her schedule really was) to reach out to me. Whenever I displayed even the tiniest ounce of doubt, she would smile and say, "Make it happen!" She encouraged me to forget the fear and go to work.

Three years later I was at Girls' State, a government camp for high school senior girls. I had set the intention to run for Governor, but once I got there and saw all of my talented debate competitors from across the state, I started second-guessing myself. I had never won a student body office, even though I'd run every year since the sixth grade. Now, here I was, running for the highest position available at Girls' State. The night before the deadline to file for office, I called my mother in tears. I told her about the girls who could potentially run against me and how I was considering backing out, so I wouldn't have to deal with the disappointment. But my smart mother, knowing how much Elaine's words had meant to me through the years, simply said, "Michelle, make it happen!"

That night, those words filled me with energy and power like never before. I filed for office, gave it my best, and won the election. It was a great experience, and I can't help but think how disappointed I would have been with myself if I had quit without even trying.

"Make It Happen" has been my life theme ever since. One reason I was drawn to Startup Princess, the organization where I now serve as managing director, was the company slogan—"Make a wish, make it happen." When it came time to name my radio show, I kicked around a lot of different options. Then it suddenly came to me in a brainstorm session—"Make It Happen"—and I knew that was it. All these years later, the message of that phrase is still just as powerful to me. It reminds me to forget the fear, forget past failures, and give it all I've got. A halfway effort isn't enough. I have to go all in and Make It Happen. I will forever be grateful Elaine was part of my original power team and cheered me on to success when I needed it.

While you can accomplish a lot with a good day planner and a great cheerleader, there's still more to the success equation. I've spent years and countless hours researching the topic. I have read hundreds of books by experts such as Jack Canfield, Brendon Burchard, Jim Rohn, Brian Tracy, Ken Blanchard, Darren Hardy, and other experts in the field of personal development. I have subscribed to *Oprah* and *Success* and every other personal development magazine I could find. Today, many of these resources are available through technology, making my interests and passion that much easier to fuel. But this learning process is more than a hobby; I often use my findings as reference points in my work.

Live events and success seminars have also served as great learning opportunities for me. I attended my first Stephen Covey seminar when I was a teenager. At a conference where the average age of attendees was 35, I was easily the youngest person in the room. It was there that I got hooked on the energy and the thrill of connecting with like-minded individuals. Live events are still among my favorite learning tools, and I love attending, speaking at, and producing them.

All my studies and exposure to success and successful people have taught me that despite the abundance and accessibility of information, there are a number of people (including myself at times) who still feel completely unsuccessful, over-scheduled, tired, and unhappy.

Why is that?

Perhaps, on a certain level, we all feel there is something else we could be doing, or worse, we feel we are missing something valuable.

How it is possible to be surrounded by an abundance of great material and resources and still feel there is some secret we're missing that only a select group of successful, wealthy people can access?

The quest for that "secret" is what has fueled my research. It has kept me up at night, fed my desire to read every new book on the subject, and led me to interview bestselling authors, CEOs, and seven-figure speakers. To date, I have read more than 25,000 pages, sat through 1,000+ hours of seminars, and watched upwards of 500 hours of programs and videos about success and business. Still, until as recently as 2011, I never really considered myself successful. Sure, I had some successes along the way, and I did not by any means consider my life a failure, but the experiences I'd had were not ones I would have included in my original definition of success.

I've come to realize that success takes on its own meaning and form for each individual. What I consider to be successful may not necessarily match what you envision success to be, and that's ok. In fact, that's one of the things I love about personal development—each of us can glean what we need at any given time. We can decide for ourselves what success means. It does not have to be a certain dollar amount, a specific family status, or a particular size of house. Success is whatever *you* say it is.

I want to help you find your own success without having to match all of the hours I've spent researching the topic. In the following chapters I will discuss the principles I've learned and applied as I've read and re-read the teachings of the greats. I have summarized my findings and distilled them down into actionable principles that you can use to simplify your definition of success and reach the next level in your own life.

In 2012 I decided to take action in my life and really work to apply the principles I had researched and shared at live events and with my coaching clients. I specifically focused on the basic principles of success. Since then, I have reached new levels in my business. In fact, writing this book is one of the many things that can be attributed to my decision to act.

The most important thing I want you to remember as you read is this:

Practice.

Success is not a destination, it's a practice. The actions we take every day, week, and month to make our dreams a reality are what determine our success and happiness. Progress, growth, and development should be a life-long pursuit. Part of that pursuit will also include failure. Failure is inevitable. The list of things I've failed at over the years would both shock and entertain you. *Everyone* misses the mark sometimes, but it's the ability to try again that builds character and success. The things I learned from my failed business ventures provided me with lessons I couldn't have gleaned from a book or classroom teachings, and my other businesses are better for them. Don't seek failure, but embrace it when it comes, and give yourself permission to grow from it.

It's interesting to note that a doctor with years of schooling and hands-on experience still calls his business a "practice." While doctors don't always get things right, their dedicated effort to medicine and wellness helps their patients. My invitation to you is to treat your life with the same care. Don't settle, dare greatly, dream big, do your very best, and if necessary, do it over and over again until you achieve success.

Past failures are not a sign that you should quit trying or stop growing. In fact, it's quite the opposite. Moments of failure and regression are often the "test" of our commitment to our life's mission and dreams. The trial separates the strong from the weak and the dreamers from the doers. Don't give up!

If you take nothing else from this book, I hope you'll glean the magic of a Make It Happen life. When we give ourselves permission to dream, create a plan for optimum results and actually put it into action, there is great satisfaction in living life on purpose and priority.

I'm sure you'll be tempted to skip around in this book. I've designed each chapter to stand alone, yet each practice is an essential part of building a high performance life and career. That said, if you do hop around, don't miss the chapter "The Plastic Bag Principle." It accurately reflects life and how we can live it at a higher level.

One more thing, before we begin. I encourage you to grab a pen and paper to take notes on the practices we discuss in this book. I've included action items at the end of every chapter. These are tasks you can use to put that specific principle into practice in your life. I imagine you will also have interesting insights as you learn more about what your purpose is and how you want to achieve your goals. Jot those down as well. Our future is only as good as our ability to apply the little nudges we receive to make our world a little better.

May your life's practice bring you the success and happiness you desire.

Now let's get started and Make It Happen!

CHAPTER 1
POSSIBILITY

"To accomplish great things, we must not only act, but also dream; not only plan, but also believe."

—Anatole France

What moments would you include in a highlight reel of your life? Do you have some favorites that immediately come to mind? Maybe you'd show a memorable birthday, your wedding, the time your children were born, or that carefree day at the beach. Take a minute to think about those moments and what made them special, and feel free to put down your book or device to ponder on the good things you've experienced in your life so far.

I always find I'm able to perceive my reality better when I'm rooted in what's good. Sure, it's easy to rattle off the problems and challenges life has brought you in the past, or talk about everything that's going wrong in your life, but that just results in a cluttered brain space. To begin anew, you have to elevate your thoughts and focus on the positive, happy aspects of life.

After you've taken a minute to think through some of your greatest moments, look to the future. Specifically, ask yourself this:

What are the deepest desires of my heart?

Your future is full of possibility, and seeing life through the lens of possibility is like removing the filters from your vision. When you eliminate the "shoulds" and "have tos" and toss out the "I can'ts" and "that's impossibles" you're left with a clear picture of what you really want. You open yourself to a future you deeply desire and, I dare say, deserve.

For most people, the mere mention of this makes their brains start churning with the negative self-talk they've been telling themselves for decades. Mixed in with that is a replay of all the so-called wisdom from naysayers trying to "give a dose of reality." If you experienced a similar reaction, it's time to get those thoughts out of your head.

Instead, try this reality: Life is not meant to be endured—it's meant to be enjoyed. Don't sit around waiting to die. Death will surely come to all of us, as will trials and heartaches, but that doesn't mean life is a death sentence. I believe that my life is mine, and it will become as good or as bad as I create it to be.

Will you join me in *living* life?

You can start by determining the desires of your heart. What do you really want for yourself? What would you like to become? What experiences would you like to have, and how will those define your future?

My father James died in 2003 of Severe Acute Respiratory Syndrome (better known as SARS) while living in China. He was one of the first Americans on record to die of the disease that ultimately took hundreds of lives. As a result, his death got a lot of media attention. As the nominated family spokesperson, I was interviewed by every local television station, many radio stations, and all the local newspapers. His death received national attention as well, and I did interviews for the *Today Show*, CBS *This Morning*, and *Good Morning America*, as well as the *Harvard Crimson* (my father received his Master's degree at Harvard), and other random outlets. Needless to say, it was a whirlwind few days from the time of his death until his memorial service.

One reporter who interviewed me also attended the funeral and did a follow-up story. After hearing my father was a member of the Peace Corps, taught English in China, and created a plan called "The Freedom Bomb" that would use literacy and education to liberate third world countries from poverty and oppression, the reporter called my father "lovably quixotic." I'm not going to lie, I had to look up "quixotic" in the dictionary, but it basically means "exceedingly idealistic." It described my father completely. He believed in world peace and freedom for all. He believed in living in full expression of self, and encouraged his family, friends, and even complete strangers to live creatively and believe in a world where anything was possible. Living and thinking that way made my dad happy.

This world needs more lovably quixotic people. We need more dreamers. We need more people who believe that wrongs can be righted and sadnesses can turn happy. We need to turn idealistic thoughts into realistic thoughts, and then we need to act on them.

Don't think small. Though you may not achieve all the dreams you set out to achieve, you'll likely find simply pursuing them brings you happiness. You'll find a sense of fulfillment on your journey knowing your dreams aren't sitting in a lonely box labeled "Someday."

Every year I choose a "word of the year" in addition to my regular goals. Previous words I've used are "Light" and "Intuitive."

At the beginning of 2013, I asked myself, "What do I want more than anything else?" The answer was simple. I wanted to be "LIMITLESS."

I wanted to be limitless in my energy. Limitless in my love—especially in my love for my kids and husband. Limitless in my faith in a higher power. Limitless in my ability to have a successful business and speaking career and grow my paychecks. Limitless in the amount I could get done in a day. Limitless in my health, nutrition, and my athletic ability. I wanted to release the limitations I place on myself and get them out of my mind once and for all. I wanted to feel limitless in my possibilities and future.

In previous and subsequent years, I shared my word with other people, but I didn't do that in 2013. Part of what I wanted to let go of were the limitations others placed on me. We all have people in our lives who make our dreams feel small. I didn't want anyone to bring me down with well-meaning comments about human limits. I simply wanted to tell myself I was limitless and live in that experience. So I kept it private and let the journey be my own.

The reality is that I know I have limitations. I know I'm not super human. I have weaknesses and shortcomings just like everyone else, and throughout the year I still had my fair share of mistakes and setbacks. I even had breakdowns and cry fests. Feeling limitless is not about having super powers; it's about letting go of weighty beliefs that keep you from your dreams. I discovered that some of the biggest limitations I have are ones I place on myself.

When I released some of those limitations, amazing things happened.

For example, in my annual planning session, and under the influence of Ann Webb's "Ideal LifeVision" program, I decided I wanted to run a half-marathon. To that point I had run a few 5K races and a 10K, but running wasn't really my thing—or at least that's what I had always told myself. I felt a pull to run a half marathon, so I decided it was time to release the "I can't run" limitation from my life. On January 1st, I registered for a half-marathon in September. I announced my intention on Facebook (because everyone knows there's no turning back once you post something on Facebook).

The training process was hard, but I began to see exactly how many of my limitations were only in my head. If I told myself "I am strong. I am a runner. I am capable and ready to run this 10 miles," I could do it. Like so many things in life, running is just as much a mental game as it is a physical one.

There were still times in those months when I wanted to quit, drop out of the training program, and never run again. Yet I couldn't escape the fact that I had committed, and though I might have physical limitations, I'm NOT a quitter. I continued my training, and I ran the race in September. For me, it wasn't just about crossing a finish line, it was about staying committed and removing limits.

Though your stories and circumstances will differ from mine, I want you to think about the limitations you place on yourself. What "I can't __________" statements are holding you back?

When it came to being limitless in my relationships, I found I understood people better when I looked them in the eye, and they understood me better as well. I tried to look at my children with limitless love, and I smiled and practiced having limitless amounts of patience. I wish I could claim a flawless track record in the parenting department, but I can't. I still snapped more than I wanted, but I also had times when I remembered to exude limitless love, and that is when the miracles happened. Just having the words run through my brain were powerful and relationship-altering.

I was blessed to see abundant results in my professional life as well. My radio show *Make It Happen* took off (it now gets more than 50,000 downloads a month—available on iTunes); I produced physical products to sell at live events; and I had some record-breaking paychecks.

I meditated and prayed for success and received energy and clarity to go to work. With those gifts, I was able to write two books. My first book, *The Time Blueprint for Entrepreneurs* (available on Amazon.com) was a #1 bestselling book in my category. It was well received, and exceeded my initial expectations. Writing a book can be hard, but I removed that limitation and created the possibility that it didn't have to take months—it could take days. When a press opportunity arose, I wanted to have this book, (previously sold as *Make It Happen*), ready for a show. I had twelve days. I worked at night and while my kids were at school. With my mind fixed upon my goal, and with incredible editors, I was able to remove my limits and release the book digitally in time for the press opportunity.

However good it felt to have the book available digitally, though, I knew it wasn't enough. After all, I was limitless! While I was in the process of exploring my self-publishing options, I sent the manuscript to an industry contact. I was hoping for feedback I could use in writing my third book, but to my surprise and delight, they wanted to publish this one. I was blown away. My dream of getting published within three to five years happened in two.

While we're on the subject of limitless business achievements, let's talk about the fact that I also quadrupled my revenue that year. To be honest, I hadn't even set a money goal. I had things I wanted to accomplish, and I kept my businesses churning, but I was shocked when I did my accounting and realized I'd earned four times as much as the previous year. Releasing limits has a way of affecting every area of your life if you open up to the possibility.

This journey naturally led me to increased prayer and meditation. With all the demands on my personal and professional schedule, I certainly needed divine help. When I put my desires for limitless ability into the hands of my higher power, I not only achieved the results I wanted, but I also became closer to Him and His will for me. Instead of thinking I didn't deserve something, I turned it over to God, and the desire didn't shrink, but was magnified instead.

Do you have an "I don't deserve that" mindset? What possibilities would open up for you if you eliminated it? What could you accomplish if you opened your vision to include what you truly desire, instead of limiting yourself with what your finite understanding says you deserve? If nothing else, what heaviness would be removed from the mental boundaries you've been placing on yourself for decades? The limitless mindset opens your world to new possibilities and new realities you wouldn't have discovered otherwise.

I received many gifts from living a limitless life, and perhaps the greatest of all was the ability to create limitless happiness. Happiness has always been a central focus of mine, but I discovered there are no limits to my ability to choose happiness, even when I don't feel like I deserve it.

LIFTING YOUR LIMITATIONS

You can have a limitless mindset and open your life up to an endless array of possibilities. The following five practices will help you get started.

First, become aware of your limiting beliefs. Chances are, you have been saying negative things to yourself for decades. Possibilities exist in positivity, so retrain your brain to be on your side. Every time you notice yourself engaging in a negative thought pattern, stop and replace it with positive talk.

Second, clear your brain of clutter. Clutter can include your negative thoughts, but it can also be simple things like to-do list items you haven't written down, or worries about home or the office. I often use "morning pages" to clear my mind. I first read about this practice in *The Artist's Way* by Julia Cameron. She talks about the importance of freeing the creative mind from clutter and recommends writing something by hand, in a stream of consciousness sort of fashion, each morning. This exercise isn't about perfect handwriting, or catching every thought, but is instead about verbalizing and then releasing your thoughts to connect you with your most creative self.

My use of this practice has evolved over the years. Sometimes I time myself, and sometimes I try to fill a certain number of pages. Though my method varies, the result is the same—freedom. I find clarity, and my dreams actually become bigger.

Another aspect of clearing your brain of clutter is finding more quiet time. We are masters at filling our lives with constant noise—music, television, Internet, and so on. Make time for yourself to be still and think without distraction, and you may be surprised what you discover.

Third, create visual cues for yourself. If you're creating a big, hairy, audacious goal or future, put visible reminders around your home. There will undoubtedly be times when your motivation meter is running low, or someone says something that knocks you down. Create visible reminders to help rally your spirits during these times.

Try using a vision board, a visual representation of your thoughts and dreams. To be honest, vision boarding always seemed a bit "woo woo" to me, but I have discovered there is actually great power in them.

I'd heard of vision boards, but I didn't start using them until 2008 when Kelly Anderson, my friend and business partner in Startup Princess, suggested I give them a try. My first board included some seemingly random things. I put a picture of a new house I wanted after carefully selecting the design from a builder I liked. I printed off a picture of money and wrote down my financial goal for the year. I found a picture of a nice digital video camera to represent video marketing and the equipment I needed to be able to do it. I cut out a picture of a magazine cover to represent media opportunities. I also included pictures of other tangible items like a desk and a flat-bed scanner. I put a picture of a tropical location, where I wanted to vacation with my husband (sans kids). And to keep me on course, I included a picture of my family in the center of my vision board, because they are my number one priority, and I know I can have anything I want as long as I include them in the process.

A few weeks after I finished the board, I had my first manifesting experience. At the time we had an old document scanner, but I really wanted one I could use to scan pictures as part of my family history. One day, I got a call from Kelly .Her voice was hesitant and she said something like, "I know this is kind of random, but I got this flatbed photo scanner to review for Startup Princess and I really felt like I was supposed to call and offer it to you."

I sat on the other end of the phone speechless for what seemed like a full minute. When I could speak, I said, "That is so weird, because I just put that on my vision board." I could almost hear the theme song from *The Twilight Zone* playing at that moment.

Now that I'm more familiar with vision boards, success stories are commonplace. With the exception of the desk, EVERY item I put on my first vision board came to fruition. My husband's work paid for us to go on a trip to Cabo San Lucas, Mexico. I saved and found the camera I wanted for video marketing. A local business magazine selected me from hundreds of nominations to be included in their "40 Under 40" feature. And the list goes on and on. It was enough to make me a believer, and I now update my vision board every year as part of my annual planning. It's something I love to watch unfold.

At the heart of vision-boarding are two main principles—deciding what you want, and believing you can have it. Some of the items on my board came to me in incredible ways, while others resulted from saving my pennies and being wise with my resources. Regardless of how each item came about, the visual reminder motivated me to put in the work to get the things I wanted. It all starts with possibility. I have a hard time looking at that board and being ho-hum about it. It fires me up and keeps me going on hard days.

If you like vision boards, you'll love another possibility tool called "Ideal LifeVision." I embraced Ideal LifeVision founder Ann Webb and her visioning tool in much the same way as vision boards—I thought she was crazy and couldn't get away from her booth at a women's event fast enough. But when I started to see results from my vision board (and nearly three years after I met her for the first time) I softened to the concept and decided to give Ideal LifeVision a whirl.

It's amazing!

It is designed to help you create your ideal life in five different areas: health, relationships, professional development, personal development, and spirituality. You write about your hopes and goals in each area using incredible detail and crystal clear clarity. Not only do you talk about what you want, but you include an action plan for how to get it. All of this is done speaking in first-person, present tense, as if you have already achieved the things you are seeking. After writing this script, you record your thoughts in your own voice set to Baroque music.

As I've already shared, your negative thoughts are the biggest deterrent to your possibilities. An Ideal LifeVision gives you something positive to combat those. Since your own voice is your most believable voice, the simple act of listening to yourself speak your goals is a powerful tool for changing your negative thoughts. After I listen to my Ideal LifeVision, I start to think in those phrases, and the thoughts inevitably lead to action.

My Ideal LifeVision brought about almost immediate results with something small, yet significant to me. I'm an avid Jack Canfield fan, and I often quote his book *The Success Principles* in my business and always recommend it to my clients. I have long admired him and I decided I wanted to meet him in real life and thank him for his work. About two weeks after I wrote and recorded that goal in my Ideal LifeVision, I got a call from my friend, Tiffany Peterson. She told me Jack Canfield was coming to Salt Lake City, and then asked, "Do you want to meet him?"

I told her about putting that in my Ideal LifeVision, and she loved how I had "seen" it before it became a reality. Six weeks later, I shook his hand.

A year after I recorded my first Ideal LifeVision, I printed it out and highlighted the things I'd seen actualized. It was fun to realize how many yellow marks were on my papers! I had achieved great things in my business, my relationship with my higher power, and with my family. And yes, I did confess to Ann Webb, who now happens to be one of my favorite friends, that I initially thought she was crazy. Now I'm hooked on the tool and wish I hadn't waited three years to put it into practice in my life and business.

(If you'd like to know more about Ideal LifeVision, visit www.IdealLifeVision.com).

Practicing possibility requires a mindset shift. It may take some retraining of your inner dialogue to Make It Happen, but stay with it. I promise you, the results will be beyond your wildest imagination.

Remember, possibilities and opportunities abound. The currency is work, and all you have to do is Make It Happen!

POSSIBILITY IN ACTION

- Does a word of the year speak to you? Brainstorm words and feelings that resonate with you about creating a life you love.
- Create a vision board. Start by thinking about some things you want personally and professionally. Find images to reflect those ideas in magazines and online. You can use poster board from the nearest discount store, or a cork board (which is my personal favorite). At the end of the year I take down my wins and put them in a "Made It Happen" book. Whenever I'm feeling low or lacking in motivation, I flip through that book and reflect on past success. It's like my scrapbook for personal development.
- Commit to writing down or verbally sharing five positive things any time you have a negative thought. Practice this for a week

(or longer) and mark your progress in retraining your brain to think in your favor.

- If you brain needs some quieting, try Morning Pages or do what my friend Marilyn Sorensen calls "inner voice appointments." That means scheduling time to be still with your thoughts and ask yourself questions like, "What do I want most?" "What makes me happy?" and "How can I grow to be the person I want to become?" The more clearing exercises I have put into use, the more I've been able to get inspiration and open up to new possibilities. Be patient; it will take some practice.

CHAPTER 2
PLEDGE

"If you want to be successful, you have to take 100% responsibility for everything that you experience in your life."

—Jack Canfield

If you could drive any car you wanted, for free, what would you choose? Now imagine someone grants your wish. You make your selection, sign the papers, and dream of roads ahead. Once all is said and done and you ask for the keys, the dealer says, "Sorry, I drive. You sit in the passenger's seat."

You're a little deflated, but you agree. After all, being driven around isn't so bad. Once you're in the car, the driver doesn't take you home, or on the road trip you've been planning. Instead, he runs his own errands around town and you're simply a passenger on his journey.

While this scenario is unlikely, the principle behind it is not. We often let others take control of our lives and dreams and dictate our course. The reality is that your future is yours, but only if you're willing to get behind the wheel.

Before you read any further in this book, I'm going to ask you to take a pledge. I want you to vow from this point on to stop being a passenger and OWN your life. I want you to be the driver that determines the car, the directions, and the destination.

This may require you to stop blaming other people in your life for things you do or do not have. It can be easy to blame your boss if you hate your job. In our current economic state, it's easy to say it's the economy's fault you can't quit and build the business of your dreams. Circumstances abound, and so do excuses, but the ultimate responsibility for achieving your dreams rests on you.

Owning your life may also mean you need to stop being offended about things people have said in the past. Don't allow others to determine your happiness level. Allowing yourself to be offended to prove a point or be right only hurts YOU. Offense often comes from a place of misunderstanding instead of truth. Don't waste your time in that space. Look forward with a strong determination to succeed regardless of the things others say and do. Their opinion of you is theirs, and it's none of your business.

My intention is not to sound harsh. I know that life is hard. I know that many of us would choose different circumstances, different paychecks, different employment, and sometimes even different family members. I want you to experience a kind of self-mastery that is rewarding despite the outcome of external things. The rest of the chapters won't mean anything if you aren't willing to own your life in every way, shape, and form. So commit now: NO MORE EXCUSES!

I remember sitting on the couch of a family friend and therapist after I got divorced from my first husband. I was quick to complain and blame my former spouse, where we lived, friends and family involved—you get the idea. Not only did she help me take ownership for my half of the divorce, she helped me keep my thoughts in check. One afternoon I was complaining about untruthful things I had heard his family say "through the grapevine," and she taught me about the "No Control Column." There are things we can control and things we can't. We can spend all day worrying about items in the "No Control Column," but it doesn't do us any good. It wastes a lot of time and brain power on something out of our control. However, for every circumstance there are things in our control on which we should be focusing and acting. We can control our attitude. We can control how we interact with others and how we choose to respond. Most importantly, we can control how we're going to move forward.

At the end of our lives we aren't granted any do-overs, so there's no room to regret things you could have done but didn't because you were too busy blaming others or circumstances. This conversation is the first and most important practice in high performance. From this point forward, own the car, take the keys, and chart your destination. Your life is yours and no one else's.

Are you ready to own your life? Not just a little bit, but all of it?

Are you ready to lose the tethers that have been keeping you tied to others in damaging and limiting ways?

Are you ready to shed past behaviors and thoughts that are keeping you stuck and unhappy?

Are you ready to open up to new possibilities in high performance?

Are you committed to creating a future and a life you love?

Say the following pledge aloud: "I (state your name), commit to owning my own life. From this point forward I choose to create a future and a life I love."

Okay then. Let's continue to Make It Happen.

PLEDGE IN ACTION

- Write down on a 3 x 5 card or a sticky note: "I choose to own my life." Put it somewhere you'll see it every day.
- Wake up every day and say, "I choose to own my life! From this point forward I choose to create a future and a life I love." Document your thoughts on the subject through a journal entry.
- Keep a pledge journal. Every time you find yourself blaming others for your circumstances, write down how *you* can overcome the challenge and responsibly move forward.
- Brainstorm the areas of your life that you have previously been blaming on outside circumstances. Next to each one, write how you can take back control of the situation and put yourself in the driver's seat.
- Next time you find yourself blaming outside circumstances for a situation or challenge, ask yourself, "How can I move forward in a positive way?"
- If you have a current challenge take out a piece of paper and fold it in half. On one side put "Control"; on the other side put "No Control"; and list the circumstances of your situation. After you've done that, go to work on the "Control" column, and waste no more time on the things outside your area of influence.

The No Control Column	The Control Column

CHAPTER 3
PERMISSION

"What you seek is seeking you."
—Rumi

The most paralyzing thought keeping you from your goals is, "I don't deserve it."

Even as you read this book, you may be saying to yourself, "But Michelle, I don't deserve that kind of success."

Oh, but you DO.

I'm going to be completely transparent. THIS was the single biggest deterrent to my goals, my future, and ultimately, my happiness. The negative scripts I ran in my head for decades have been very hard to quiet and retrain.

As an avid debater, I often lamented about the lack of a professional debate team. We have professional football and hockey, so why not debate? That would have been the perfect life path for me. Someone once said to me, "You could be a motivational speaker." That satisfied me, and I responded, "Sure. Someday."

Well, life happens. I went to college, and although I was on the debate team, there was no "professional speaking" degree, so I ended up focusing on marketing and public relations. I loved it. I worked for advertising agencies and a television station, and even started an underground newspaper with some friends.

When I got married and had kids, "someday" felt very far away. Shortly after the birth of my second child, I started to get healthy again and lose some weight. Through the course of reshaping my body, I also reshaped my confidence, my businesses, and my future. One day, the thought came to me, "I think it's time. Someday is today."

Until that point I had been doing some public speaking here and there by invitation, but on that definitive day, I decided it needed to become a priority. I hired a coach to help me put my speaking business together, and when she asked me what I wanted most, I responded, "I see myself as a highly-paid, highly sought-after speaker who gets paychecks with commas in them."

All at once, an amazing thing happened. When I actually said the words, "I'm a speaker!" it felt like the universe aligned with me and started to rally on my behalf. It was amazing. Doors started to open, invitations came out of the blue, and resources became available to me to produce my website, speaking materials, and videos. It was almost as if those "gifts" were waiting for me to say, "I'm ready."

I was humbled and grateful, but almost at the same time, resistance crept in to my thoughts. Like that negative friend or family member who's always telling you to "be realistic," my mind, (and truthfully, some of my friends) went a little nutso.

"You don't have the talent for that."

"You can't do that; you're a mom."

"Who are you kidding? There are lots of people out there who are better speakers than you are."

I started to worry about what others would think of me, and how they might judge me for my aspiration. It all cast a dark cloud over the experience and felt very heavy to me. As a recovering people pleaser, I was ready to throw in the towel, just so I could make someone else happy. In hindsight that seems so silly, but at the time it was very real.

At a women's business event in Salt Lake City, one of the panelists said, "If everyone in your life agreed, what would *you* choose?" The amount of clarity that came from that simple question made all the difference in the world. I realized my dreams and aspirations were mine, no one else's. I couldn't wait to make my move until everyone gave me their stamp of approval. My desire was the only validation I needed. And the same is true for you.

Whose permission are you waiting for so that you feel it's okay to have what you want?

In this instance I became keenly aware that I was waiting for an engraved invitation and everyone in my life to come on board for the ride. I was waiting for *everyone* to say, "You've got this, Michelle. You will be an awesome speaker, and I'll do anything you need to make it happen."

As nice as that would be, such support rarely happens. Few people will understand your dreams, and even fewer will rise to the occasion and be your constant cheerleaders. It's not because they're jerks—it's just because they are probably too wrapped up in their own dreams and battling their own self-doubt to lend you the support you seek. For me, in the absence of permission from others, I found approval within myself, and from the one source that mattered most.

I know many of you believe in a higher power, and though we may call it different names, for me, God is a powerful influence in my life and business. I seek His counsel in every endeavor, and this one was no different. I wanted a sign. I wanted His permission to proceed in building a speaking career. I knew the path was going to be challenging with two little kids at home, and I knew I wanted to be with them as much as possible, so working full time wasn't an option I was willing to consider. I prayed and meditated to find a way to make it work. I didn't know how it could be done, but I knew He could help me, if it was His will.

While I was still waiting for my (now divine) engraved invitation, I started to see something incredibly powerful. Despite the resistance I felt from myself and others, doors began to open for me. I saw this as the most important sign I needed: God wanted more for me than I wanted for myself. I realized how important it was for me to decide and get in alignment with Him.

What I wanted then, and what I still want, is to be happy. I want to want what I want, and I want that to be okay. As I think about my life's purpose and mission, I'm not living up to who I am if I wait for permission from others and stuff my dreams away in a drawer somewhere.

What are you hiding away that would ultimately make you happy?

It doesn't matter if you want to be a stay-at-home parent, or a brain surgeon, or a gold medalist—it's your dream. Give yourself permission to achieve it and you'll find greater joy in your life. That joy will spill over into every aspect of who you are and who you show up to be. Passion and purpose are contagious.

What surprises me most about being on this path and sharing through social media what I'm up to as a speaker, or as I wrote this book, is the number of people who say, "I'm so proud of you for going after what you want!" I can feel their genuine support, and yet I'm equally surprised when they express, "I wish I could do that."

I'm here to tell you that you can. And you need to.

Although this statement is often wrongly attributed to others, Marianne Williamson is famous for saying:

> Our deepest fear is not that we are inadequate. Our deepest fear is that we are powerful beyond measure. It is our light, not our darkness that most frightens us. We ask ourselves, "Who am I to be brilliant, gorgeous, talented, and fabulous?" Actually, who are you *not* to be? You are a child of God. Your playing small does not serve the world. There is nothing enlightened about shrinking so that other people will not feel insecure around you. We are all meant to shine, as children do. We were born to make manifest the glory of God that is within us. It is not just in some of us; it is in everyone and as we let our own light shine, we unconsciously give others permission to do the same. As we are liberated from our own fear, our presence automatically liberates others.[1]

Are you ready to step into the light and wave your own flag? Are you ready to live your dream and obtain the validation you desire while giving others permission to do the same?

The world needs more dreamers, more high performers, more people who aren't content settling for mediocre. It's time to stand up and create the future and life you love.

Still not ready? I've created a "Permission Slip" for you. Take action on your dream and Make It Happen!

---

1 *A Return to Love: Reflections on the Principles of "A Course in Miracles,"* Ch. 7, Section 3 (1992), p. 190.

PERMISSION IN ACTION

- Print your own Make It Happen Invitation by downloading the *Make It Happen Workbook* at www.speakmichelle.com/books.
- Print the word "Permission" and place it on your vision board.
- Make a list of positive, firm responses that put you back in the driver's seat to your future when naysayers and dream stealers try to take control.

CHAPTER 4
PURPOSE

"Let us not be content to wait and see what will happen, but give us the determination to make the right things happen."
—Peter Marshall

From the time I was very little, my dad would earnestly ask me, "What is the meaning of life?" As a kid, I didn't really understand the question. Sometimes I ignored him. Sometimes I answered with random kid thoughts. We have one of these conversations recorded in an old home video. Dad asked me (then twelve years old), "What is the meaning of life?" and I responded confidently and happily, "Babysitting!" Over time, my answers changed, and when I eventually realized there was no "right" or "wrong" response, I started digging deeper.

As I side note, my dad asked everyone that question. He was known for it. He had a deep desire for everyone to know the answer to that question for themselves. Although he has passed away, I often wonder what he thinks of me writing a book like this, and I don't doubt for a minute that his repeatedly asking one simple question had a lot to do with where I am right now.

Ultimately, I believe the meaning of MY life is to be happy, and to choose happiness despite whatever challenge comes my way. But it also goes a little deeper—where possible, I am determined to help others find that same joy.

Do you know what your purpose is? Last year I read *The Compound Effect* by *New York Times* bestselling author and publisher of *Success* magazine Darren Hardy. In the book, Hardy talks extensively about finding "your why." I've reflected a lot on that concept this past year because I feel many people never come to understand their "why," or in other words, their purpose.

When I hired my first success coach, Tiffany Peterson, to help me launch my speaking career, she took me through a powerful exercise to help me discover my "why." As I answered a series of simple questions, I became so full of passion about my purpose that I started doing laps around my dining room table. I wasn't having any new realizations about what I wanted to do with my life, but verbalizing my purpose was energizing and empowering.

What are you passionate about? When you're talking with your family and friends, what lights up your eyes, puts a smile on your face, and gets you excited? Is it love, business, money, sports, politics, success, health, or happiness? Whatever the topic may be, do you get just as excited about your business? I hope so, and if you do, you are probably pretty motivated by your purpose. However, if you don't, it may be time to reevaluate some things.

One thing I love about working with entrepreneurs is that most are driven by at least one of two things: they are either super passionate about what they do in their business, or they are super passionate about what their business provides for them in the way of lifestyle, steady income, a roof over their heads, etc. This passion is critical to happiness and success, because even when you are passionate, running a business can still be tiring and hard.

If you already know your life's purpose, congratulations! If not, take some time to discover it by answering the following questions or using the worksheet in the *Make It Happen Workbook* found at www.speakmichelle.com/books.

1. What motivates me to do what I do every day?
2. What do I want to change about my world?
3. Whom do I want to influence, and why?
4. What am I most passionate about?
5. What do I love to learn about?
6. What activities make me the happiest?
7. What do I want to accomplish before I die? What would I regret not doing?

Within your answers you will find the beginnings of your purpose. But asking the questions is just one piece in the discovery process. To complete the process, connect with God, or your higher power. Meditate, pray, and ask for guidance as you figure out your life's work.

Once you understand your purpose, summarize it, write it on a 3x5 card, and place that card somewhere you will read it every day. My card is taped to my bathroom mirror, and at times it has been my saving grace. When doubt and vulnerability creep in (and that happens more often than I would like), I look at that card, think of my purpose, and pray, a LOT. Getting rooted in my purpose and mission makes all the difference in how I perform, and it helps me navigate the invitations I receive to help with projects, events, businesses, etc. If an invitation supports my purpose, I can accept, but if it doesn't, I know I need to pass.

YOUR PURPOSE VS. YOUR MESSAGE

I recently attended an event for coaches and trainers where the facilitator asked the question, "What's the difference between your purpose and your message?"

In that instant, something clicked for me that hadn't clicked before: Your purpose is your life's mission. Your message is how you sell it.

My purpose, my mission, is to help individuals choose happiness and fulfillment in every stage of life, despite the challenges that come their way.

So why do I work at business consulting for entrepreneurs? Why do I host marketing events? Why do I write books about success and high performance?

First of all, if I told you I was a "happiness coach," you would probably dismiss me and tell me you don't "need" that. Second, my own set of life experiences as a small business owner, and my education in marketing, allow me to be a resource to others who are walking the path of entrepreneurship. Finally, since we spend the majority of our hours working, it's a great place to start in the quest to find fulfillment and joy in the everyday. It's my desire to help people not only make a living and thrive at doing what they do, but also come to love their life's work. After all, happiness is not found in a paycheck. That's just an external symbol of tasks completed and a job well done. Happiness is found in the doing every day.

Again, if you're still looking to find your purpose, that's ok. Some people find it when they are young, while others discover it later in life.

The worksheet in the *Make It Happen Workbook* at www.speakmichelle.com/books will help you with this process.

Once you find your purpose, live it with passion! Happiness and passion are contagious. Be brave. Be bright. Be passionate.

Your life's purpose doesn't have to be saving the world. It could just be saving your world or your kids' world. Your life's purpose could simply be enjoying each day. There are no right or wrong answers, and your purpose doesn't have to be a certain size or shape in order for it to be right for you. Every person has unique gifts and talents to share, and they are all important and needed.

Consider this quote from the movie *Hugo*[2]:

> Everything has a purpose. Clocks tell you the time. Trains takes you to places. I'd imagine the whole world was one big machine. Machines never come with any extra parts, you know. They always come with the exact amount they need. So I figured if the entire world was one big machine . . . I couldn't be an extra part. I had to be here for some reason. And that means you have to be here for some reason, too. (Hugo Cabret)

Everyone has a purpose, and the sooner you discover yours, the sooner you can begin sharing it with the world. Discovering and living your purpose not only brings you happiness, but it touches, blesses, and inspires those around you.

Peter Shankman was speaking to a group of inner city youth when one asked him how he became so successful. I loved his thoughtful and powerful response:

> I told him . . . he has to realize the majority of people he'll meet in his life will spend tons of time finding excuses not to do

2 http://www.rottentomatoes.com/m/hugo/quotes/.

something, and not enough time finding ways to get something done. I told him I've never seen myself as successful, I'm just someone who sees opportunities where others see doubt, and I don't like excuses, I prefer finding a way. I told him that the next time he has a choice between finding an excuse not to do something or finding a way to do something, find the way. That's success.

It's time to stop making excuses, and start doing. That is what makes high performers unique. What are you waiting for? As Grace Hansen said, "Don't be afraid your life will end, be afraid it will never begin." It's time to get moving and Make It Happen.

PURPOSE IN ACTION

- Spend some time in nature each week and fully enjoy it by leaving your phone and other technology at home. Connect with your higher power and the beautiful place you live on a regular basis.
- Practice meditation and prayer. Make it part of your daily routine morning and night. Connect with your source to find and live your purpose.
- Keep a journal, and note insights about yourself and your life as you live your purpose.
- Occasionally revisit your purpose statement and check in with your current values and goals. Some wording may change over time as you gain more experience and clarity. A purpose doesn't have to be etched in stone; it can be ever evolving, just like you.
- Put your purpose statement in your phone with a reminder notification so it pops up each day.

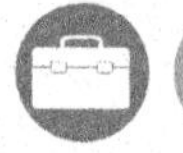

CHAPTER 5
PLANNING AND MY TAKE ON GOALS

"He who fails to plan, is planning to fail."
—Winston Churchill

It's fun to say the word "plan" at speaking engagements, or when working with clients, because it often elicits audible groans.

Many people, especially creative types, shy away from, or flat out avoid planning and goal-setting because it's not really glamorous or fun, it may seem rigid or restricting, and frankly, it takes effort. But I always tell my clients that "plan" is the four- letter word for success. High performers know this, and they find power in a plan and thrive on the execution and ultimate success of seeing it through to completion.

I totally geek out over planning. I've spent a lot of time learning the tricks and science behind it, and I attribute essentially all of my business success to good planning and powerful, purposeful execution.

My world would completely collapse without a solid planning system. I currently have two children under the age of seven, and run three businesses from home. I made it a goal from the time I started having kids to spend as much time as possible with them before they were old enough to attend school. For that reason, I don't have a regular nanny or send my kids to daycare. Instead, I trade with friends when I need to attend meetings or speaking engagements. This has made for a packed schedule, and often conflicting priorities, but I have found that with a solid plan I have the time to work on my business without sacrificing my family or a meaningful personal life.

People often ask me how I am able to do so much. I tell them the key is to have a planning mindset and the proper tools. The following practices include the two main planning tools I use—The Time Map and The Goal Map—as well as other tips that I have discovered help me keep a proper frame of mind and work smarter, not harder.

PLANNING PRACTICE #1: MAKE PEACE WITH THE CLOCK

Sydnee, one of my clients, is a social media coordinator for a large networking and information site. She is awesome at her job. She is very social both on and offline, and loves connecting with people. She initially hired me to help her create systems and routines to manage the multiple deadlines she was juggling.

Like many of you, Sydnee called herself "a creative," and told me planning wasn't her thing. Yet, when I pressed her, she conceded she felt overwhelmed, tired, and "off." Plans are not intended to ruin creativity, nor are they only successful for the analytical. Planning is a way to overcome the overwhelming feelings and make the most of your time.

Please don't get caught up in the lie that planning just won't work for "someone like you." Sure, it may not be second nature for everyone, but it can be learned, and anyone can find great success in creating plans.

Start the planning process by making peace with the clock. The clock is not a ticking time bomb. Though time is a fleeting resource, and we all wish we could have more of it, we need to acknowledge that it is the great equalizer in the world—we all have the same number of hours in the day.

I've always been motivated by the quotation from H. Jackson Brown, "Don't say you don't have enough time. You have exactly the same number of hours per day that were given to Helen Keller, Pasteur, Michelangelo, Mother Teresa, Leonardo da Vinci, Thomas Jefferson, and Albert Einstein."

That list contains amazing creative individuals, all of whom were able to accomplish grand things in the same number of hours you have in your day. Time is either your greatest asset or your greatest liability in life and business. Time is the currency of your goals and dreams. Stop fighting the clock and start investing your time well.

If you need to, change the words for things. Later on I'll share a system I use called the Time Map. I use the word "map" because people are so averse to the word "plan" that map sounds more like a fun journey. If that still doesn't work for you, cross out the word and call it whatever you want. Call it "My Awesome Future" or "My Life, My Way." If you're about to gag yourself with cheesiness, stay with me. The point is not to get caught up in semantics or let your past feelings affect your future. While you're making peace with the clock, make peace with the words and phrases you associate with time management. They aren't out to get you.

PLANNING PRACTICE #2: OWN YOUR DAY

Either you run your day, or your day runs you. I quit working my full-time job after the birth of my first child, and I was very excited to move my side business, Doodads Promotional Products, to the front burner. Although I knew that with an infant, it wouldn't be a full-time endeavor, I was looking forward to giving it more attention, and I was excited to bring home a paycheck on my terms.

I soon learned that my now "free days" were quickly packed with caring for the baby, fulfilling church responsibilities, attending mom-and-me playgroups, helping family and friends, and a million other activities. Time went by quickly, and I wasn't as productive as I needed to be. I had mistakenly assumed that since I was not punching a clock for someone else, I would be able to manage my own schedule with ease. I was wrong. I had great to-do lists, a full wall calendar, and very little productivity. Every day, my husband would come home from work and supportively ask me how my day was. I often replied, "My day was not my own." I would then launch into a long, dramatic story (he's a great listener) about how the neighbor needed help with something, or how I got caught on the phone with a client for too long, or how I had an emergency with an order that had to be handled.

This routine went on for two years, at which point I had another baby and two additional businesses. Then, I found myself sitting in a live event where the facilitator was talking about taking full responsibility for your life. I'd always prided myself on my ability to own my life and my future, but just then, the words, "my day was not my own" echoed in my head like a haunting chant.

This was a huge "aha moment" for me.

I realized that in a very real way, I was giving up my day and blaming other people for my lack of structure and planning. If I was going to help so-and-so down the street, I needed to choose that, and own my choice, instead of blaming them for my ever growing to-do list. Or, I needed to learn to say "no" a lot more. The solution was actually a combination of the two. I began making better decisions about what I did and did not agree to, and made a commitment that I would begin owning my days.

We talked about this in the chapter "Pledge," so I'm not going to into great detail here. I do want you to consider the ways you displace responsibility for your planning and productivity. In what ways are you blaming others (or your "creative nature") for time slipping away each day? What needs to happen to get you back on track to creating a life you love?

PLANNING PRACTICE #3: COMMIT TO A TIME MANAGEMENT SYSTEM THAT WORKS FOR YOU

I've tried a number of different calendars and productivity devices in search of what worked best for me. I've used a Franklin Day Planner, a wall calendar, a desk calendar, a Palm Pilot (remember those?), a Google calendar, an app on my phone, the calendar on my phone—you get the idea. I love and embrace the digital world on many levels, but last year I realized that when it came to planning, I was a pen and paper kind of girl. I switched back to this old-fashioned method, and I couldn't be happier.

That's why I don't advocate a specific program or system. The best system for you is the one you will *use*. If you currently aren't using one because you don't feel like you have found a perfect fit, I would encourage you to implement the system you like most for now. You can always change systems. However, going without a system at all is like working without a safety net, and relying on your brain alone is a dangerous endeavor. Please don't give up on calendars because they "aren't your thing." The minutes tick by and the days vanish, whether you like it or not, so figure out how you can function with some tool at your fingertips.

The Time Map

I first learned about the concept of a time map from a business associate. While the system didn't completely fit my needs at first, over time I was able to tweak it and make changes. Now, I've found it not only works for me, but it also works for many of my clients—both the analytical and the creative ones.

Why a Time Map?

If a geographical map guides you from point A to point B on land, then a Time Map shows you how to get from where you are to where you want to be in terms of your schedule and desired results. Brendon Burchard tells us, "Success is scheduled." Whether you are a busy business professional trying to master your work and personal priorities, or a stay-at-home mom who wants to feel more fulfilled and have time to work on your dreams, the Time Map can help you schedule your days *one week at a time.* Best of all, the Time Map can easily be integrated with whatever system you're currently using, be it Google Calendar, iCalendar, a wall calendar, you name it.

What Is Block Time?

Block time is a specific chunk of time set aside for a certain task or activity. The Time Map relies on these time blocks that are placed in your schedule just like appointments. For example, each week, I schedule a marketing time block on Monday afternoons from 12:30 PM to 2:30 PM. During that time, I review my marketing plan, make a list of things to do that week for marketing, plan posts for social media, review upcoming email launches, and handle whatever else needs to be done for marketing that week. I do not answer the phone, check my email, check social media, or do anything else that does not pertain or that will distract me from the task.

If you've never used block time, I encourage you to give it a try. If you are an entrepreneur, your time blocks might include the following activities: marketing, administrative tasks, content creation, networking, event follow-up, education, product fulfillment, accounting, phone calls, emails, etc. Bigger tasks obviously require bigger blocks of time (2–3 hours), while smaller tasks require smaller blocks of time. Whatever your industry, the time blocks can be customized to fit your needs.

What Goes on the Time Map?

Each of your most important roles should be included in your Time Map. Want to spend more time with a specific child? Schedule it. Want to dedicate more time for marketing or product development? Schedule it. A Time Map can help you focus more on your roles, and less on your to-do list as you take all the tasks you do (or should do) on a weekly basis, as well as your calendared appointments and activities, and fit them into one organized schedule.

LIFE PRIORITY SYSTEM TIME MAP WEEK OF:

	MONDAY	TUESDAY	WEDNESDAY	THURSDAY	FRIDAY	SATURDAY	SUNDAY
Before 5:00							
5:00 AM							
6:00 AM							
7:00 AM							
8:00 AM							
9:00 AM							
10:00 AM							
11:00 AM							
NOON							
1:00 PM							
2:00 PM							
3:00 PM							
4:00 PM							
5:00 PM							
6:00 PM							
7:00 PM							
8:00 PM							
9:00 PM							
10:00 PM							
11:00 PM							

MICHELLE McCULLOUGH

If you'd like to learn more about how I use a Time Map as an entrepreneur, I discuss the system in greater detail in my book, *The Time Blueprint for Entrepreneurs—The 5 Categories That Will Help You Work Smarter, Not Harder.*

PLANNING PRACTICE #4: SET GOALS AND WORK TOWARD THEM

In the movie *Alice in Wonderland*, Alice finds herself in an unusual place. Unsure as to which direction she should head, she seeks guidance from the Cheshire Cat. He wisely asks her where she wants to go, but when Alice isn't sure, the Cheshire Cat tells her, "Well then, it doesn't matter which way you go." Setting goals and managing your time works much the same way. That is, it doesn't much matter how you manage your time if there isn't a goal in sight.

Goals are the motivation for progress and high performance. Sure, you could take life one day at a time and never hope or dream of something more, but high performers know better.

Each of us has an innate, human desire to be challenged. We are driven by it, and we often learn from our experiences to set a target and hit it. Even if we don't reach our intended goal or destination, we gain strength in trying. Getting an education, building a savings account, becoming a bestselling author, and climbing the corporate ladder are all worthy goals, as are providing for your family, expanding your knowledge and expertise through reading, and choosing to find happiness every day. Whatever your desires, they can be fully realized in a well-stated goal with a plan to achieve it.

However, many people have had less than stellar experiences with goals. Can you relate?

Take New Year's resolutions for example. If you ask me, they are recipes for failure and disappointment. According to a study done by the University of Scranton[3], only 8% of people who set resolutions actually keep them and reach their desired goal. That means 92% of us are NOT reaching our goals, and probably feel like failures because of it.

---

3 Source: University of Scranton. *Journal of Clinical Psychology* 12.13.2012

Don't get me wrong, I love the idea of renewal and resolve. Both are powerful principles of high performers. However, New Year's resolutions tend to fail because:

- *What we have in resolve, we lack in planning.* We often forget that planning is a big part of achieving any goal. If you want to lose 10 pounds, don't just say it, create a plan with action items to help Make It Happen.
- *We feel we can only create powerful change at the beginning of a year.* Did you fall off the diet wagon on January 15? The negative side of your brain might tell you all hope is lost. With that mindset, you then have to wait 350 days to try again.
- *Renewal and change can happen at any time, but for some reason we get it in our heads that we have to wait in order to set a new goal.* You'll be a lot happier if you think of *each day* as an opportunity to renew your interests and goals.
- *They establish a pattern of failure in our brains.* Did you set a resolution last year to lose weight, stop smoking, or organize the garage? Did you accomplish your goal? Every New Year we're reminded of all the things we set out to do last year and never did. This makes us start to lose credibility with ourselves.
- *They deliver an un-engraved invitation to depression.* As the failure of not reaching our goals sets in, we add the experience as another rung on our "failure ladder," and soon we stop even giving ourselves a chance.

Forget about New Year's resolutions. Instead, resolve each day to be better than the day before, and set motivating goals to help you create the life of your dreams, one day at a time.

THE MISSING PIECE IN GOAL ACHIEVEMENT

In 1981, George Doran created a goal framework called S.M.A.R.T. Doran said that every goal should be:

Specific
Measurable
Attainable
Realistic
Timely

I love the principles Doran outlines, and I've used this framework in my own teaching. However, I think Doran is missing one key element of goal setting—your "why." With that in mind, I share the Doran-McCullough goal framework, which I call S.M.A.R.T.Y.:

Specific
Measurable
Attainable
Realistic
Timely
Your Why

Keeping your purpose in mind and staying grounded in your passion will take you through the dips you encounter on the path to achieving your goals and becoming a high performer. Consistently remembering the motivation for setting the goals in the first place will help you keep going when times are tough and temptations and obstacles abound.

WRITE DOWN YOUR GOALS

According to success expert Brian Tracy, only 3% of Americans actually write down their goals[4]. Research has also found a correlation

4 Brian Tracy: http://www.briantracy.com/blog/general/planning-your-year/.

between those who write down their goals and those who actually accomplish them.

We have many fleeting wishes in our head—everything from wanting a better physique to accomplishing more in our careers, and a million things in between. Some of those wishes are short-term, while others require a long-term commitment. How is your brain supposed to go to work on any of them if you don't narrow the field and create an area of focus?

My creative brain is constantly churning with new business ventures, product offerings, activities for my kids, trips I want to take, items on my to-do list, and more. When I narrow down my ideas and turn them into written goals, amazing things happen and I accomplish them. Focus is an important key in goal achievement, and another way you can set yourself up to succeed as a high performer. Writing your goals down is a way of creating that focus.

GOAL GRADATION

Generally speaking, I love BIG, HAIRY, AUDACIOUS GOALS that excite and motivate me, but tackling those goals can be overwhelming. That's where goal gradation comes in handy. Goal gradation is the process of breaking a big goal down into several smaller, more attainable ones, which will ultimately help you achieve something that may have initially seemed impossible.

Goal gradation may also be appropriate if you're a perpetual New Year's resolution breaker, or if you have a habit of working on goals half-heartedly. It isn't an excuse to aim low, but it is a way to create little victories, build confidence, and establish a pattern of success. If you're a sales employee, and the goals you've set in the past aren't motivating you, or if you're consistently missing the mark with them, lower the goal, hit it, and then move on to a bigger goal.

It sounds simple, but those who are feeling a little low in high performer pride would do well to embrace the practice of goal gradation.

GOAL MAP

My favorite tool for goal achievement is the Goal Map. (A free downloadable copy can be found in the *Make It Happen Blueprint Workbook* at www.speakmichelle.com/books.) Similar to a geographical map and the Time Map, the Goal Map shows you how to get from where you are to where you want to be in terms of your goals. Perhaps you want to write a book, finish a big task, save a set amount of money, take a trip, or tackle a home improvement project. It's one thing to dream it, but it's another thing to actually DO it. The difference between our visions and the outcome is the PLAN we put in place to Make It Happen! A goal map acts as that plan, and uses the following steps to see goals through to fruition:

Step 1: Define Your Goal or Project

What do you want to accomplish? Be sure you write it down.

Step 2: Define Your WHY

Why do you want to accomplish this goal in the first place? Again, write it down. When worry or self-doubt creep in, you can reread your "why" and get back on track. Is your bathroom growing mold and making your kids sick? That's a great reason for a renovation. Are there women struggling with the same issues you face, and you have a proven framework that can help them? Write it down. Write down why you've been prepared and chosen to write your book. Let your "why" drive you today, two weeks from now, and as long as it takes to reach your goal.

Step 3: Choose a Deadline

What is a realistic timeframe for you to accomplish your goal? It's a curious thing, but projects will get done in the amount of time we give them. If you want to write a book in six months, it will take you the full six months. If you give yourself a year to finish your personal history, it will likely take you a year. Our brains are hard-wired by the calendar, and since earlier in this chapter you made time your friend, it won't be hard to choose a realistic date in the future. Remember, all good goals have a plan, and deadlines are part of any good plan.

Step 4: Choose an Accountability Partner

Accountability is key to success. You need a cheerleader, but not a taskmaster. You need someone who will take the journey with you and keep you on the right path. Choose carefully. Sometimes spouses or friends are the right choice, and sometimes you need someone else who can be objective and supportive. Once you have chosen an accountability partner, share your goals with them, and be clear as to the type of support you need.

Step 5: Chunk It Down and Work Backwards

Take a look at your goal and create four mini-milestones between now and your deadline. If you're writing a book, perhaps Milestone One is creating a title, defining your audience, and laying out your table of contents. Milestone Two might be creating chapter summaries. Milestone Three could be writing the first five chapters, and Four could be writing the final five chapters. See how that works? The little milestones act as a type of goal gradation, and make it easier to accomplish what may have originally seemed unattainable. With your milestones mapped out, work backwards and create mini-deadlines for each one.

Step 6: Create Your Actions List

An actions list is a glorified to-do list. Brainstorm all the little actions you must do to achieve your goal. Get granular and specific. The individual tasks should be things you can accomplish in an hour or less, and they should be just as measurable as the goal itself.

Step 7: Add Your Goal Map to Your Time Map

This is where the magic happens, and I completely geek out at this point. Schedule time in your calendar each week to work on your goal, your milestones, and your action list. Execution is truly where you take your goal from an idea to reality.

Take some time to try using the Time Map and the Goal Map. You may discover they fit your needs completely, or you might decide to make adjustments for your specific circumstances. Whatever the case may be, I can't emphasize enough the necessity of using some sort of planning system.

PLANNING IN ACTION

- Find a fun clock to put in your house that helps you feel creative and abundant, instead of limiting.
- Print out a copy of The Time Map and try implementing it for three weeks. (Remember, you can integrate it into any calendaring system you're currently using.) You can get a copy of the Time Map in the *Make It Happen Workbook* http://www.speakmichelle.com/books.
- Schedule evaluation time at the end of each week to ask yourself what did and didn't work and make adjustments as needed.
- For a week, take note of your most alert and energetic times of the day. Schedule your creative tasks during those times each week.

- Make planning and scheduling fun by creating a list of rewards you can give yourself for staying on plan.
- Use the Goal Map this week to write down your top five goals. Feel the power of written goals, and powerful execution plans.
- If you're still struggling with planning, go back and re-read the chapter on possibility. There are some tools for creative thinkers that may be just the ticket. But again, don't discount planning just because it hasn't worked for you in the past.

CHAPTER 6
PRODUCTIVITY

"Dost thou love life? Then do not squander time, for that's the stuff life is made of."

—Benjamin Franklin

Now that we've thoroughly covered planning, it's time to tackle productivity. Planning and productivity go hand-in-hand, but they are distinct and different from each other. You can't be productive without a plan. A plan is what you're going to do, and productivity actually ***makes it happen***.

THE FOUR TIME TRAPS

As a business coach and someone who loves productivity, I have found there are four common time traps that tend to drain people's days and their paychecks. Do you recognize any of these in your own life?

Trap #1: Failure to Plan

We sufficiently covered planning in the previous chapter, but I'm including it again here because it is the number one time trap. Many people skip the planning step in hopes their productivity and awesome to-do lists will make up for it. Don't make that mistake. If you skipped the previous chapter, I encourage you to go back and get familiar with it. Understanding the mindset of time management and getting the tools to help you succeed will allow you to make time your friend.

Trap #2: Distraction

Early settlers were challenged to build communities using their physical labor. Although there are still those who perform physical work today, the digital age has led to a society of office workers and paper pushers. This has given new challenges to high performers. Now, instead of battling nature and the elements to be productive, we must contend with email and social media notifications on our computers and phones, text messages, social media feeds with endless information about our friends' lives, not to mention barking dogs, chatty coworkers, the latest blogs, news and gossip sites, and a million other distractions that come our way. Plus, we have ideas coming to us faster than we have the time or ability to act on them.

Distraction can kill the best laid plans. A study conducted by Basex Research found the average employee in corporate America spends 2.1 hours a day on interruptions[5]. Think about it, that's 28% of your workday, or ten-and-a-half hours a week! I do most of my consulting

5 http://www.basex.com/press.nsf/0/E53F4C6142D119A6852570F9001AB0EC?OpenDocument.

with small business owners, and I wonder if their percentage is actually higher. Without a "boss" encouraging them back to work, it's easy to get sidetracked on winding paths and down rabbit holes.

If you want to be a high performer, you need to become aware of the distractions that are stealing your productivity. At this moment, you may not be conscious of what those are, but if you pay attention over the next week, you'll start to notice all the ways you get distracted from your greatest priorities at home and at the office.

Awareness is the first step. The second step is cutting those distractions down—and FAST. I'm not just talking about cutting them from work time, either. You should be mindful of the things that interfere with your relationships with your spouse, kids, or friends. How often do you get interrupted during important moments?

You may want to try these to decrease or eliminate distractions from your day:

- *Turn off the email and social media notifications on your phone and computer.* Instead, schedule times in your day to check them in a purposeful way. This may be incredibly hard at first, but if it's high performance you're after, you'll need to trade distractions for focus and productivity.
- I allow myself to *check email three times a day.* This helps me manage my time, and ensures I don't get caught up in things that are not a priority. I also allow myself only three daily social media check-ins—for five minutes each! Sure, I miss responding to a personal tweet from time to time, but I've found that the interrupted task is often more important than the notification. I won't allow my relationships to erode over a tweet or Facebook status update. What may or may not be an "email emergency" only takes my focus away from what is likely a more important work project.

- *Post office hours on your door.* Whether you work at home or at the office, let your coworkers, babysitter, kids, spouse, or anyone else know your schedule. Set boundaries for work time, and honor your personal time with the same dedication.
- *Don't answer your phone during your block times.* When you're in the middle of a project, let your calls go to voicemail. Basex Research also found that when someone is distracted from a specific task, it takes an average of 25 minutes to get back to it. Honor your brain and the focus it needs to complete your tasks and you'll be more productive than you have ever been.

Trap #3: The Misdirection of Multitasking

Trying to do two things at once is a recipe for failure. The time has come for you to give up your "Multitasker of the Year" award. For a long time, I wore that award like a badge of honor. I was often complimented on my ability to do two things at once, so I continued on the path of not only trying to do it all, but trying to do it all at the same time. When I finally woke up to *presence*, my world changed. I was more productive and profitable in my businesses, and my relationships began to thrive.

It may seem counterintuitive that doing only one thing at a time would be more productive, but the reasoning is simple—I can't give my clients the attention they deserve if I'm crafting an email, answering the phone, or checking social media updates at the same time. Likewise, I can't be the rock star mom I want to be if I've got my head in my phone instead of in the game I'm playing with my kids. Trade multitasking for focus and presence, and you'll find a practice of high performance that will rock your world.

Trap #4: Failure to Delegate

At some level, each of us needs to delegate or outsource some tasks so we can spend time on the things that matter most. As a busy professional, what things can you give others so you can do what you do best and spend more time with the people in your life you care about? Maybe you could hire a house cleaner, get your shirts laundered, have someone handle your shipping and receiving or bookkeeping, and, well—you get the idea. You can start the delegation process by creating a list of things that can be outsourced at a rate cheaper than your hourly wage. This will give you a good idea of how much time you can free up to accomplish revenue-generating activities.

If you, like me, are also a mother, how can you accept offers of help from others so you can be less taxed in your important and honored role? This might take a little extra thought, but using your creative brain and keeping your unique circumstances in mind, think of ways you can get help so you can create more presence for and focus on your kids.

For additional resources on why and how to delegate, my eBook *The Time Blueprint for Entrepreneurs* has two full chapters dedicated to the subject. It will help you bring more focus into your business.

TACKLING TO-DO LISTS

You probably keep some form of a to-do list. I'll admit it, I'm a compulsive list maker. I love them. I love to write things down so I remember them, and I love checking off completed tasks even more. But despite their generally helpful nature, to-do lists can also bog us down and cripple our productivity. If you find your to-do list is consistently growing instead of shrinking, the following tips may help you tackle it and get it under control.

1. Keep all of your tasks in one place on a single list. It doesn't matter if you keep your list digitally, or on paper, but it does matter that you have only one list, that you know where that list is, and that you check it regularly. Don't write things on sticky notes, the backs of receipts, or random pieces of paper. Trust

me, I know the consequences. Like your time management tool, the best system for keeping track of your to-dos is one you'll use—the reminders on your phone, pen and paper, a fancy app, or whatever works best for you.

2. Don't rule your day by your to-do list, rule it by your schedule. For example, schedule marketing time into your day, then work only on the marketing items on your to-do list during that time block. Batch similar tasks and block out time in your schedule to complete them.
3. Take a look at your current to-do list and determine what can be delegated or outsourced to someone else. Being a high performer doesn't mean you have to do it all, but it does mean you use your power team to accomplish more in less time, and focus on what you do best. If you do outsource some tasks, make sure you schedule "managing" into your Time Map.
4. Some items are "do once" tasks, while others fall into the "do regularly" category. It's important to keep track of both. Break "do regularly" items into Daily, Weekly, Monthly, and Annual to-dos, and then take them off your list and put them on your calendar. Set notifications for these items and block out time to get them completed. To accomplish everything on your "do once" list, schedule one-hour time blocks in your day under "Admin" time, and check off as many as possible.
5. Stop beating yourself up over missed deadlines and growing to-do lists. Either delegate it, do it, reschedule it, or make peace with it, but don't let it become a 24/7 guilt fest.

It's also okay to schedule and take down time when needed. Don't plow through to the point of a breakdown. Take vacations, and enjoy mini-breaks doing the things you love like athletics, reading, crafting, etc. If necessary, schedule them. High performance is not about giving up things you love—it's about being incredibly productive with your responsibilities and work time, so there's time left over to do the things you enjoy.

NEXT LEVEL PRODUCTIVITY FOR HIGH PERFORMERS

I introduced this principle in the chapter on Planning and in Tip #4 on tackling your to-do list. However, I think it needs a little more attention before we move on. High performers don't just have powerful to-dos—they have routines and practices that keep them at the top of their game. This is where planning and productivity align to bring top results. While some projects are only done once, most activities that contribute to our personal and professional success lie in practices we invite into our life on a regular basis.

If you don't have your business mapped out in an action plan, go back and review the chapter on Planning. What items are on your actions list for your physical health? Relationships? Personal Development? Decide on the items that need to be done frequently, and make them daily action items. Less frequent items go on your weekly actions list and should be assigned a specific weekday to complete them. Schedule your tasks and implement them into your Time Map as discussed in that chapter.

Like planning, if you need to change the verbiage or reframe past experiences to be more at ease with the practice, I encourage you to do so. I see each day as a game in which I prove how much I can get done. With a little planning and a lot of productivity, I create days that are purposeful, efficient, and effective so I can conquer my goals and Make It Happen.

PRODUCTIVITY IN ACTION

- If your to-do list is in multiple places, schedule time this week to consolidate it to one list.

- Look at your list and put a D next to any task that can be outsourced or delegated.
- Turn off your email notifications while you work. If someone really needs to reach you, they can call.
- Turn off your social media notifications and check social media during scheduled or blocked times. I have yet to hear of a social media emergency.
- Create your ACTION list that has your daily, weekly and monthly activities.
- Schedule time for the people you love. Make time with your spouse, kids, family, or friends just as important as a meeting with a client. Then, when you're with them, put down your phone, close your laptop, and be present.
- Create a sign for your office door that says, "I'm in the middle of a project. Unless it's an emergency, please send me an email or leave a voicemail message and I'll get back to you when I'm finished. Thanks for helping me be a high performer!"
- Go to the office supply store and look at the notebooks and journals. Find a book you love that makes you feel happy and energized and can also double as a to-do list. Sometimes legal pads do the trick, but in my case, a decorated journal puts a skip in my productive step. Or, if you're a fan of working digitally, find a To Do app for your smart phone. Either option is great as long as you are checking it on a regular basis.
- If you're an entrepreneur create, post, and stick to your own "office hours." Aside from the occasional emergency, get your personal life back by sticking with a reasonable schedule. If you're currently working 60–80 hours a week, learn to "own" delegation as much as you own your business. I've seen more businesses fail because of the owner being overwhelmed than I have because of financial instability.

- Look at your to-do list and separate out the daily, weekly, and monthly tasks, as well as yearly activities and planning. Brainstorm any additional things you do on a regular basis, and then schedule them all on your calendar.

CHAPTER 7
PEACE

"If there is to be any peace it will come through being, not having."
—Henry Miller

For aspiring and ambitious high performers, busy can be normal. We have a lot to do, we've organized ourselves to do it all, and we quickly run from one thing to the next.

My good friend Melanie (who also happens to be the editor of this book) once told me, "Did you know every time I ask you how you're doing, you say, 'Busy but good'?"

"Busy but good" is my normal, but perhaps I shouldn't broadcast it whenever someone asks how I'm doing. There's an interesting and potentially heavy energy about it, and I was grateful she brought it to my attention. I'm now much more conscious of how I answer that question.

I'm not an expert in stillness, but I have been trying to practice more peace in my life. As someone who wants it all, and tries to go after it, I once thought including quiet time in my routine was a good idea. Now I find it's more than that—it's critical to my success.

It's in quiet moments that I receive inspiration on how to be a better parent, spouse, and business owner. It's in quiet moments that I refuel my tank and find energy to take on the day. When I've taken time to invite peace, I'm able to respond without snapping, even amidst project deadlines and kid mayhem. And creating peaceful moments every single day helps me achieve consistent levels of high performance.

Here are some tips for filling your high performance life with peace:

First, think "simplify and savor" rather than "get it all in and rush." It sounds obvious, but reminding ourselves to keep that focus is the first step to clearing the clutter and eliminating the extra noise in our head. If this is a struggle for you, place peaceful pictures and words in your workspace and daily surroundings to remind you to quiet your mind—even in the middle of the day.

Second, make "inner voice" appointments. I'm going to get a little woo-woo here, so if that's not your thing, skip the next tip on the Power Up and Power Down routine (one of my favorite success practices).

I learned this tip from my friend Marilyn Sorensen (www.marilynknows.com), who shared some of her gifts with me this year. It was a pleasure working with her—she enlightened me, helped me see my strengths and weaknesses, and taught me how to optimize my gifts for the greater good. As part of this, she encouraged me to schedule "inner voice" appointments a few times a week.

To do this, I block out time in the middle of the day to just sit and think. I love meditation and prayer, and I continue to do those morning and night, but I also hold daily inner voice appointments. Sometimes the appointments are only ten minutes, and sometimes they're as long as thirty. I often have to do a little brain dumping and clearing first, so that I can truly be still, but I'm completely converted to the practice. I've realized my brain needs some time to process the day and my future without the distractions of the phone, the kids, and the notifications on my computer. These appointments let me clear my brain and ponder questions about how I should proceed on a specific project or address an issue at home.

This world is overrun with technology—devices and social media platforms, phones that call, text, and play music, and televisions and shows, just to name a few. So much noise. Our brains need quiet time to relax, and sleep alone isn't enough. I encourage you to try it for three weeks and see what works or helps. You might be surprised.

Third, when things get really out of whack, take some extra time to reconnect with nature, with your Higher Power, and with your soul. We are ever-evolving beings, and as we learn and grow, we find new insights and understanding. From time to time I feel as though my priorities are out of balance and I'm not completely myself. When that happens, I return to my Source and go deep within myself to find out what needs to change. I can get a lot of information by simply asking myself:

1. What's working?
2. What's not working?
3. What needs to change?

These questions help me evaluate my life and the course I want to chart for the future. In fact, they can help in many areas of life.

Consider your relationships. What's working? What's not working? What needs to change?

What about the marketing efforts for your small business. What's working? What's not working? What needs to change?

Now think about your physical health? What's working? What's not working? What needs to change?

You get the idea. Keep those questions in your high performance toolkit and they will help you break out of practices that are holding you back. They can also help you open up to practices that will move you forward confidently.

Fourth, make sure you read the next chapter on the Power Up and Power Down routine. It's by far the best way to bring peace and order into a busy life—so important it deserved its own chapter.

When I share these practices with others, I often hear, "I feel guilty any time I take time for myself." You aren't doing anyone any favors by sacrificing you. Investing a little time to bring peace into your life will provide big returns in every area. You too can enjoy the benefits of a well-rounded and peaceful you. Stop putting yourself last and Make It Happen!

PEACE IN ACTION

- Read the next chapter, "Power Up and Power Down."
- Schedule an "Inner Voice" experience with yourself. See what insights come to your mind when you find quiet time in the middle of the day.
- Take time to walk, hike, or ride a bike. Enjoy the world's amazing creations. Sometimes we get so used to the buildings, vehicles and noise that we miss opportunities to grow, expand, and think. Walk on grass in your bare feet, eat your lunch in a park, or plan a weekend when you can go for a walk or a hike. Nature is nurturing and peaceful.
- Put the three evaluation questions on a 3 x 5 card and reference them whenever you feel stuck: What's working? What's not working? What needs to change?

CHAPTER 8
POWER UP AND POWER DOWN

This practice is an important part of bringing peace in my busy world, but because it's so powerful and so important, it needed its own chapter.

The Power Up and Power Down Routine is a *must* for high performers. Just as airline passengers are instructed to put on their own oxygen masks before helping those around them, high performers know they must take care of themselves in a nurturing and energizing way that brings order, clarity, and peace. It's easier to handle the stresses of the day when you start with a full tank. If you're a high performer running on empty because you never have time for yourself, the Power Up and Power Down routine will help you begin and end each day with *you.* You'll start with a full well of love and nourishment that you can share with others because you have filled your own first.

I can't take credit for coming up with this idea in its basic form, but I've tested and tried it in a few ways, and it's imperative that I pass along the ways I've implemented it as one of my favorite and most effective success practices.

Perhaps you've already heard of a "Power Hour." It's basically an hour in the morning full of planning, reading, and preparing for the day. After reading about this practice a few years ago, I realized that since I was 12 I'd been doing something similar—the fifteen minutes of morning planning recommended by Franklin Day Planner. Eventually I stretched that time to an hour. When I made a commitment in 2011 to do it with regularity, it changed my life.

Later that year I started coaching with Tiffany Peterson. She introduced me to her "Morning and Evening Ritual," which added even more focus to my routine.

I've combined and modified all of these philosophies to create what I call the Power Up and Power Down routine. I like the energy around starting my day with positive re-charge, and then putting body and mind to sleep at the end of the day. As we'll discuss in the "Physical Health" chapter, sleep is a crucial part of your high performance abilities, and preparing your body and mind for that is important. The Power Down helps me quiet my thoughts and put my world (and my brain) to bed.

POWER UP

In the morning, before I do anything else, I get my heart rate up with some physical exercise. Sometimes this is a little walk around the house to get a glass of water, or sometimes it's some jumping jacks. Anything will do, really. I usually do my full workout after I've been up for a while, so this is a simple movement to wake me up physically and mentally.

After my physical activity, I review my goals, listen to my Ideal LifeVision, look over my vision board, and flip through my "Why" cards. I think about my husband and kids individually, and get centered on how I can show up for them. I read something inspirational or motivational, and then meditate and pray. This gets me ready to face the day.

An important thing I learned from Tiffany was that this doesn't have to take a whole hour. If your time is limited, it can be fifteen minutes, or you can spend more time if you have it. The key is to do it before any other distractions enter your day. That means you do it even before logging in to Facebook or checking your email, because those things take you into other people's issues, questions, and drama. If you have children, it's best to do it before they wake up so you have some quiet time that doesn't involve their agendas.

POWER DOWN

At the end of the day, I start my Power Down routine by writing five things I'm grateful for in my gratitude journal. Next I review my schedule for the following day so I don't end up lying in bed wondering what time my dentist appointment is, or if my meeting with a key client got moved. Then, I read a little for business and a little for pleasure before I close my day with something inspirational to reconnect me to my Source.

It's important to do all of this in a technology-free zone so the brightness and images aren't burning into your brain right before you go to bed. Turn off your laptop and stop looking at your Instagram feed. You'll rest easier when you steer clear of it before bed.

My Power Down routine always happens, but I sometimes notice after a vacation (or even a long weekend when I've slept in), it's easy for me to fall out of the habit of my Power Up routine. However, I can always tell the difference in how my day runs when I miss it. If I wait until the phone rings or my kids are awake to start my day, I feel like I'm always a step behind, so it doesn't take long for me to get back in the habit.

POWER UP & POWER DOWN ROUTINE

Power Up - Morning

- Physical Activity
- Review Goals & Purpose
- Inspirational Reading or Practices
- Motivational Reading (Plasticity Time)

Power Down - Evening

- Gratitude Journal
- Review tomorrow's Time Map
- More reading - motivational or recreational
- Inspirational Connection

Begin and end your day with you so you have the energy and mental fortitude to deal with the issues and challenges of each day.

Like all success practices, it's important not to throw in the towel if you have a hard time implementing this new routine, or even if you sometimes forget to do it. Keep at it so you can see the long-term benefits. It's worth it. It's true, you'll probably have to get up earlier than you used to, but since you're putting your brain to bed well, you should sleep better and wake up more energized and ready to embrace the day, despite the earlier time. Be committed to you and make the appointments with yourself morning and night non-negotiable.

I tell my coaching clients that they don't have to do the Power Up and Power Down routine every day—just the days they want to be a high performer.

POWER UP AND POWER DOWN IN ACTION

- Commit to a Power Up and Power Down routine for about 90 days. After a week or two you can feel free to make adjustments to the order or amount of time you're spending on it. Some people need more time in the morning and evening than others, and many people need more time in the beginning as they start this practice, but then it tapers off over time. Stick to it, and chart your insights.

- Create space on your nightstand for your Power Up and Power Down tools. Right next to my alarm clock is my gratitude journal, my day-to-day journal, my scriptures, a motivational book, and lots of pens. Have what you need at arm's length. Or create a separate space in your home for this practice, but with all the same tools.
- When you get up, do something physical. I don't do my exercise for the day, but I do something to wake up my body. Something as simple as a walk around the house, getting a glass of water or doing some quick jumping jacks.
- What books have been on your "must read" list for a long time but you haven't had time to get to? Buy one, or check one out from the library, and start reading it during your Power Up and Power Down routine.
- Find a journal or notebook that has a cover that inspires you and put it by your bed to use for a nightly gratitude journal.
- What personal and professional development reading will help you be at the peak of your industry? How can you incorporate them into your Power Up and Power Down routine?

CHAPTER 9
PERSISTENCE

"Most of the important things in the world have been accomplished by people who have kept on trying when there seemed to be no hope at all."

—Dale Carnegie

I'm a recovering sedentariest. Never heard of it? That's probably because I just made it up.

Movies, popcorn, chocolate, and my couch are pretty much my favorite things. Ever.

However, after experiencing a momentary lapse of judgment, I decided to put all of those things aside and commit to running a half marathon. Do you have any idea how much running is involved in training for a half marathon? A LOT! It didn't take long for me to get sick of it, and just when I did, the mileage started to increase. Sigh.

During one weekend of training I decided to move my Saturday "long run" to a Friday night. It was the first time I had ever run eight miles, and I made the decision to run from point A to point B instead of doing a crazy long loop, or an out and back course where you run half your distance and then come back the same way. A friend suggested I run down the paved canyon trail near my home, and that sounded like a great plan to me.

Since I was running alone, I grabbed some mace, and hit the trail. It was a beautiful, cool night in the canyon, which made the challenging run fairly enjoyable. I felt pretty safe as I passed many other runners, and people riding bikes and longboards. Then, around mile seven, I realized I hadn't seen anyone for a while. With the sun setting and an underground tunnel approaching, my overactive imagination got the best of me and I decided I should switch my mace from "locked" to "ready," just in case.

Then it happened. About half a mile from the end of my run, I tripped on an uneven part of the trail, and my thumb accidentally hit the mace's spray button. A small amount came out on my finger and somehow made its way to my face. At first I laughed. Crazy stuff like this happens to me all the time. My face began to sting a little, but I was almost able to finish my run with the song lyrics "I'm a hazard to myself. Don't let me get me. I am my own worst enemy," going through my head.

Then, as if on cue, as soon as I hit 7.8 miles, my face caught fire. My eyes started stinging and I couldn't see. I stumbled to the car to get my phone, but I couldn't see the numbers to dial. I thought about asking Siri to "Google mace remedies," but I wouldn't have been able to see the responses even if she found something. I managed to call my husband, but there was no answer. Then I called my mom, who wasn't at home and was unable to look up a remedy. Finally, I opted to go to a nearby gas station where I spent the next twenty minutes bawling and flushing my eyes out with soap and water to get a bit of relief.

Now, I could have easily taken this little setback as a sign that I should not run. In fact, too often that's exactly what we do. We hit a bump in the road and decide to stop pursuing our dreams. We tell ourselves "it's not meant to be," or "I don't have what it takes," or make up any number of other self-sabotaging excuses to abandon the mission, purpose, or goal we'd set out to accomplish.

If you're ready to give up, don't. I refer to these experiences as "trials of fate," because they are simple events sent to test our conviction. Some trials of fate come in the form of financial obstacles; others look like negative thoughts; and they can even appear as "helpful" friends or family members who give bad advice or quash your dreams. Don't let these trials convince you that you don't deserve the desires of your heart.

Successful people experience setbacks. In fact, successful people experience failures—lots of them!

Check out this powerful quotation by Calvin Coolidge:

> Nothing in the world can take the place of persistence. Talent will not; nothing is more common than unsuccessful men with talent. Genius will not; unrewarded genius is almost a proverb. Education will not; the world is full of educated derelicts. Persistence and determination alone are omnipotent. The slogan "Press On!" has solved and always will solve the problems of the human race.

A success coach turned dear friend of mine, Tiffany Peterson, put it another way when she said, "Persistence trumps talent."

What a relief!

All too often we discount our ability or our dreams with incorrect assumptions such as:

"Other people can do ________ better than I can, so I shouldn't even try."

"My parents grew up in poverty. I grew up in poverty. I'm not meant to earn more than this."

Maybe you can relate or perhaps your story looks a little different from these examples. Your past does *not* determine your future. The choices you make from this point forward determine your future. What are you going to choose?

Kelly King Anderson, my current business partner and the founder of Startup Princess, has always said, "You have every gift, talent, and ability that you need to succeed." Some call this an assumptive statement that doesn't take into account one's limitations. I think we should all start assuming that we can do more and Make It Happen.

Persistence is the easiest way to spot a high performer. High performers don't let simple things discourage them from doing their best. They don't let a little failure here and there keep them from moving forward. In fact, they see failure as a teacher and seek to learn from it, but they don't dwell on it or internalize it as a character flaw.

WHAT ARE YOU MEANT TO LEARN FROM YOUR FAILURES?

I've started, sold, and grown more than eight businesses in the last 15 years. Some of those businesses were clear failures, but they were also the best teachers. My three current businesses thrive because of what I've learned from the failures and setbacks I've experienced. In the end it's not what happens to you that defines you, but rather your ability to turn those trials into triumphs.

Returning to class after failing a test builds your character.

Following your passion and starting another business, even when the last one bankrupted you, shows you and the world you don't give up easily.

Making another call after getting rejected with a vehement, "No!" builds strength and confidence and gets you one step closer to hearing "Yes!"

Continuing to run after a mace mishap makes you stronger—and more careful with your weapons of self-defense.

Pastor Steve Furtick wisely stated, "One of the reasons we struggle with insecurity is that we compare our 'behind the scenes' to other people's highlight reel." Though some people are more public than others about their trials, everyone is having them. The world needs high performers like you to set the example of how to accept failures, dust off, and move on with your head held high. Whether you face a business failure, a divorce, a missed opportunity, a lost sale, a fumbled business presentation, or all of the above, own it, learn from it, and envision a successful future and then go Make It Happen.

PERSISTENCE IN ACTION

- Are there any past mistakes or failures you can review to find learning experiences? Don't dwell on what happened, but rather learn what you can, let go of the guilt, and move forward.
- Print out Tiffany Peterson's saying, "Persistence trumps talent." and put it by your computer or somewhere you will see it when you need inspiration. You can find this free in the *Make It Happen Workbook* found at www.speakmichelle.com/books.
- Create routines in your business that encourage persistence. How do you stay "top of mind" in the eyes of your potential customer? How do you encourage repeat business from loyal customers? In what ways can your sales team follow-up on old

clients and inquiries? Persistent and strategic marketing will ensure that when they are ready, they think of your company.

- Have you given up on key people in your life? Consider using more persistent efforts to cultivate better relationships with work associations, friends, and family members.
- Keep the lock on your mace in the "off" position until you're certain you'll need it.

CHAPTER 10
POSITIVITY

"Happiness is the object and design of our existence."
—Joseph Smith

Look on the bright side.

The glass is half full.

See the world through rose-colored glasses.

If life hands you lemons, make lemonade.

Laugh, and the world laughs with you.

Happiness might just be my favorite topic. My collection of quotes and clichés on the subject could probably wallpaper a stadium. But happiness is something that often eludes many of us. We know we want it. We know it's possible. What we don't know is how to get it.

There are plenty of happy people in the world, so what's their secret? How do they cultivate and create lasting happiness? Everyone would probably answer that question a little differently, but for me, happiness lies in creating rituals that help me choose happiness on a daily basis. Yes, happiness is a choice, and it may require practice to be able to make that choice consistently.

Too often we blame circumstances for our unhappiness. We tell ourselves, "I'll be happy when ________________." That blank can be anything. I'll be happy when I get a better job. I'll be happy when I finish school. I'll be happy when I have kids. Or even, I'll be happy when my kids are grown. What's your most common "I'll be happy when ________________" mantra? What are you waiting for? High performers know how to find happiness and joy at any moment.

My mother, Candy, is one of the best examples of happiness in my life. She used to keep the Chinese symbol for happiness in our home and around her neck. She always displayed quotes about happiness, and would often teach us how to find joy every day. It wasn't until I was older that I understood the power of her message. As a divorced, single mother of four children, one of which had Asperger Syndrome and required a lot of extra attention and resources, she had every excuse to be sad. Yet she always chose to hold her head up and see the best in any person or situation. As a result, she made a great life for herself and her kids and set an example that will always stick with me.

A friend who attended my bridal shower taught me another great lesson about positivity. As every guest went around the room and shared a piece of marriage advice with me, I heard many good tips like, "Don't go to bed angry," "Read books together," and "Make sure you both know what's happening with the family finances." Then, one of my dearest friends, who had more than 20 miscarriages and two tubal pregnancies before being able to adopt four beautiful children, said with a quivering lip, "Find happiness in every stage of life. I've wasted a lot of time being sad. Don't do that." Her advice pierced me, and I vowed to always find joy in life.

Looking on the bright side isn't always easy, but I do try. So much so that when my friends talk to me about issues and life problems, they often stop me before I open my mouth and say, "I know, Michelle, I'm sure you can find a bright side."

Lest you think my life has always been roses, I will tell you I was married (for the first time) at twenty-one. Things went south faster than I could have ever imagined, and 16 months later, I found myself divorced. I learned some great things from that marriage, and I recognize the powerful role it played as a key chapter in my life. Even so, it was one of the darkest and saddest periods I've ever experienced. My marriage was broken, and I felt fairly broken myself.

It was during that time that I read Sarah Ban Breathnach's book, *Simple Abundance*. It's a beautiful book about finding and experiencing rich abundance in life. In it, Breathnach recommends keeping a gratitude journal. I remember thinking, "If she knew what was going on in my life, she would understand it's not the right time for me and a gratitude journal." But after reading about it in nearly every chapter, I eventually consented, almost in an attempt to prove her wrong.

Her challenge was to write five things every day for which you're grateful. In the beginning, the things I wrote were simple and surface level. I was grateful for my health, a roof over my head, a car, dinner, and a paycheck—even though it was a poor college-student paycheck. As the days progressed, I began to open my eyes to the world around me, and I discovered I was receiving little blessings every day. I had been so caught up in my woes that I was missing the things being sent to preserve me. When I started to keep track of them, I found more, and more, and more, and realized that on my worst days, friends had called, mysterious visitors left laundry soap and postage stamps on my porch, teachers appeared, and coworkers lifted my spirits. These things had been happening all along, but until I truly opened my eyes to the good, I missed the mini-miracles all around me. I still have that first gratitude journal; it is one of my most treasured possessions. Miracles are all around you, too. You can see them if you look. I still keep a gratitude journal, and it helps me every day.

Some people look at gratitude journals as something only girls or softies use, but that's not the case. Many high performers understand the importance of recognizing the good in the everyday. A couple of years ago I attended Brendon Burchard's *Experts Academy.* One of his guest speakers was nine-time *New York Times* bestselling author David Bach, who wrote *Start Late, Finish Rich*, and other financial books. He talked about how he keeps a gratitude journal. I was thrilled to find a successful, influential man who values looking on the bright side.

When you look for the good in your world, you find it. It's as simple as that. On the other hand, when you look for the bad, you find that, too. Unfortunately, too many of us spend our time looking for and dwelling on the bad. When I interviewed media and marketing expert Peter Shankman for my radio show, he issued a challenge asking everyone to "make a commitment to stop spreading the drama." We can do this in social media, in our homes, in our communities, during lunch meetings, at the water cooler, you name it. Let's all stop spreading the drama, and turn our attention instead to the good and positive things happening all around us.

WHAT IF I HATE MY JOB? THE TALE OF TWO WORKERS

We spend so much of our lives working, that our jobs can be a big point of stress for us. It's my mission to help more people love what they do and be high performers doing it.

At one point I had the opportunity to work as the Public Relations Director for an attorney who did a lot of public speaking and sold information products at live events. We handled all of the order-fulfillment at our office, which meant we did a lot of work with a major shipping company. On days when we had large outbound shipments, the driver who serviced our route would complain about the amount of work we created for him. It always made me wonder: wasn't this his job? We couldn't possibly be the only office on his route that had him pick up packages, could we? Yet his behavior was always the same.

I've often thought about that delivery guy and wondered how many people are unhappy with their jobs. Then I compare his behavior with that of Richard, my favorite employee at a store I frequent. Richard is the happiest cashier I've met. He goes above and beyond the call of duty, is always cheerful, always willing to show you where something is, and takes pride in his work and the customer service he provides. I would guess he is in his 50s, and I know many people might look down on a job working at a discount store, but not Richard. He owns it. He's happy with it, and he spreads his happiness to make the customers happy, too.

Are you like Richard, always happy and helpful doing what you do? Or are you more like the delivery guy, grumbling over the required elements of your job? If you're in a job you hate, why do you keep doing it?

When I talk about this at live events, people come up to me after and explain that it's hard to find a job, or that they have to work where they do because it's close to home, or they have benefits. I understand how difficult it would be to feel tied to a job you don't love. In such circumstances, it would seem there are two choices: either get a new job that will make you happier, or make the best of the job you have. It's as simple as that. If you can't change your circumstances, you can change your outlook. Try writing down the things that are good about your job, and focus on those. When you focus on the good, more good will come of it.

CAN MORE MONEY MAKE ME HAPPIER?

As an American, it can be easy to equate success and happiness with money. However, I've learned over the years that money has very little to do with it, and I often have to remind myself to redefine success in terms of what really matters—wealth of relationships and the opportunity to share my mission and messages.

When I was fourteen, my mom took our family to Mexico for a family reunion. We went primarily to do humanitarian work, and we spent most of our time painting and cleaning an orphanage and building an extra room onto a family's shack.

Both were emotional and humbling experiences, but the memory of the family still moves me today. They had eleven children and two parents living in a house the size of my living room. The kitchen was in the same room as the bedroom, and with only two double beds, it was unclear where everyone slept. The walls were made of tar paper, and the dirt floor inside the house was the same as the ground outside the door. They used a hole twenty feet from their home as a bathroom, and washed their clothing in a pond behind the house that was so murky I couldn't see the bottom. When the children were seven years old, they dropped out of school and started doing odd jobs in town to earn money. All of the family's earnings were pooled together and used to buy food and bare necessities.

We gave them so little, but they acted as if the four-foot by four-foot addition we built on their house had turned it into Buckingham Palace. On our last night with them, they made us dinner and presented a program in which one of the daughters sang an American hymn in Spanish, "You Can Make the Pathway Bright." They left an impression on me I hope I never forget.

That family chose happiness. They didn't have wealth, electricity, or running water, but they were happy anyway. That night, and still in my memory, they were bright, shining lights of joy that made everyone smile. They were grateful for every little thing they had, and they loved each other. Their gratitude and love made their small home ooze with happiness.

So what's your excuse? No doubt you have challenging circumstances and experiences of your own, but there is also good all around you. How can you change your outlook to make positivity your priority?

The always insightful and soulful Danielle LaPorte was a guest on *Make It Happen Radio*. She and I have been connected through Startup Princess since 2009, and it has been an honor to watch her business grow and see her evolve into the person she has become. On my show we talked about the release of her book, *The Desire Map*, and she shared how feelings are the start and "the heart of the matter." She went on to say something incredibly powerful:

> Being happy and in a state of joy is the best way you can be of service to the rest of us. When you vibrate in that way, when your frequency is about joy, you are kinder, your brain is firing 'mo better,' you're more fun to be around, you're infinitely more productive and you're going to be more helpful and generous. So get happy and you will serve humanity.

THAT sounds to me like rising above whatever challenges have been holding you back and keeping you from being happy. THAT sounds like high performance.

If you don't think your positivity has any effect on your job, relationships, or even strangers, spend twenty-four hours committed to being happy all day long. Make it your "science project" and watch what happens. If you want to increase your own happiness, increase the happiness in someone else.

I know that some of you reading this are in deep despair. I know the challenges you face are real. There is real tragedy lurking in our hearts and homes. If you are in the midst of such a situation, consider this: in that same interview, I asked Danielle the question I knew many of you would ask if you could, namely, "What advice would you give to those people who say, 'I can't possibly be happy right now. You have no idea what I'm going through'?"

Her response was poignant and deep. Danielle said,

> I feel for you. I get it. Maybe you can't be happy right now, but the thing you can do right now is start to believe that your happiness is worth it and valuable. That it's actually a priority. That you deserve it. Then you can start to consider how you *want* to feel. You may be feeling taxed and overburdened and there are rough things happening and finances, parents, kids, illness . . . . How would you rather feel? Don't worry about getting out of your circumstances, and don't worry about solving it. Just get in the state where you can say, "I would prefer to feel energetic." "I would prefer to feel calm." And then find one thing you can do tomorrow to feel that way.

We'll talk about this more in a later chapter, but know that simple changes can bring great results. Decide today to allow yourself to feel how you want to feel and then DO the things that will help you feel more positive and joyful. (If this conversation with Danielle LaPorte is calling to you, you can download and listen to the whole show by going to http://bit.ly/MIHDanielleLaPorte. You can see all of our past *Make It Happen Radio* shows by going to http://www.speakmichelle.com/podcast.)

It can be hard. I know.

I also know you can do hard things.

When days are hard, and when it feels easier to fall back into old practices, remember that high performers don't settle for average and don't take the easy route. They don't just desire happiness for themselves and others, they take steps to Make It Happen!

POSITIVITY IN ACTION

- Start your own gratitude journal and write down five things you're grateful for every day. Just try it.
- Try the positivity "science project" for one day. Commit to being truly happy for a whole day and see how it affects your relationships, your work environment, and even the strangers you encounter through the day.
- Next time you find yourself complaining about work, take time to make a mental or written list of all the good things about your job.
- If you don't like your job, make a choice. Decide to appreciate it and acknowledge how it helps you and your economic situation, or schedule some time this week to update your résumé and begin searching for something new. Don't waste another minute working somewhere you don't love.
- Print the "Choose Happiness" graphic from the *Make It Happen Workbook* and post it somewhere you will see it on a regular basis.
- Make a commitment to stop posting your drama to social media. Use social media as a tool to spread positive and uplifting messages to your followers and friends.
- Re-read the section with Danielle LaPorte and ask yourself, "How would you rather feel?" and then find at least one thing you can do tomorrow to feel that way.

CHAPTER 11
PLASTICITY

"If you are not willing to learn, no one can help you. If you are willing to learn, no one can stop you."

—Unknown

The Merriam-Webster online dictionary[6] defines "plasticity" as "The quality or state of being plastic; especially: the capacity for being molded and altered."

High performers know that in order to succeed AND outperform the competition they must be willing to be molded. They must be teachable and have the capacity to learn and grow. That's why most high performers keep a finger on the pulse of their industry and dedicate time to personal and professional development. They never assume they

6 http://www.merriam-webster.com/dictionary/plasticity.

know it all, or that past success will guarantee future paychecks. High performers understand it takes work to continually stay at the top of their game.

Additionally, high performers are open to constructive feedback from peers, bosses, and employees.

Instead of refusing or trashing the feedback you receive from others, I suggest you try a new approach. I tell this to each of my new clients, and I'll say it to you as well—your job is to be a sieve (think colander or strainer) and not a sponge or a rock. To do that, take in all of the information you read in this book and others. Hear and listen to every word of feedback you receive. Soak up knowledge from industry publications and leaders. Then, do what sieves do—separate the information. You can't internalize everything, and your growth process will be slow if it doesn't include learning from others; so keep what is valuable and let go of the things that don't resonate with you.

Your ability to grow is directly related to your willingness to learn and be moldable.

Over the years, I've kept tabs on two companies where I used to work. Each company has a smart leader at the helm, but one has a hard time keeping up with industry trends, while the other makes it a point to stay at the forefront. As a result, the former is still doing the same things with the same clients and hasn't experienced any real growth, while the latter company has become a top provider of digital technology, and services clients across the country.

What will it take for you to keep up in an ever-changing, ever-growing world?

We all wear many hats—we're people, professionals and many of us are parents. Regardless of the roles you play, plasticity is important! Here are some ways to apply this principle in a few different roles.

IF YOU'RE A PARENT

Subscribe to a blog or magazine on parenting that matches your values and views. Read books about parenting that you're drawn to and apply some tactics in your home and family and see if they resonate. Talk to friends about what works and what doesn't work. But at the end of the day, I think it's important to read a little, make parenting a priority, and then do the things that work best for you and your kids. All the books in the world won't make up for how you know and understand YOUR kids.

IF YOU'RE A PROFESSIONAL

The best place to start is within your specific industry. If you sell tires, keep up with the latest models and their performance. If you're in the coaching world, pay attention to the programs and offerings other coaches are creating. If you're in the software and application industry, study user interface, design, and functionality.

High performers read and subscribe to trade publications, frequently check key blogs or sites, and attend networking events and annual conferences with other industry leaders. Being an expert means having an awareness of the trends and taking action accordingly.

You may want to consider becoming a member of industry trade associations. This is a great way to keep up on trends and stay connected to industry leaders. Search online for national organizations and see if there are local chapters you can attend. Also, look ahead for their national conferences and make plans to be there and participate on whatever level you can. In time, you'll figure out how you can contribute to your chapter or the association as a whole. Watch and learn first, then contribute your own genius at appropriate times and places.

Keeping pace is not just about how you create products and structure your business; it's also how you market to your target consumers and prospects. That's why it's important to keep up with target market trends as well. To do this, you need to read what your customers read, listen to what they listen to, and watch what they watch. Find out what they want and need from your company, and learn how you can reach them through advertising media. If you spend time studying your target consumers and are still unclear as to what they want, ask them. More often than not, they will be happy to tell you, and grateful someone is trying to understand and meet their needs.

A third area to keep current on is innovative trends and tips for your specific job title. Are you in sales? Then read, listen to, and devour information about sales—even if it doesn't pertain to your specific industry. If you're an entrepreneur, read about small business ownership and growth. Discover how others made their mistakes and their millions, and learn from them. Look for key people to follow in your favorite social media outlets, and make reading on the subject a priority.

IF YOU'RE A PERSON WHO WANTS TO OPERATE AT HIGH LEVEL

Never stop learning. Read books on subjects that interest you, read and learn about culture, art, science and even read fictional literature. Choose a subject outside of your profession to learn about on an annual or seasonal basis. You'll find that your ability to be moldable comes not just in knowing your professional life, but expanding as a human as well.

Sounds like a lot of learning, right? It is, and at the outset you might be wondering, "How am I supposed to keep up with keeping up?" I'm glad you asked. Here are some simple tips to help you manage your plasticity:

SCHEDULE TIME EACH WEEK FOR INDUSTRY LEARNING AND PERSONAL DEVELOPMENT.

If you work for yourself, about 5–10% of your work week should be spent on actively learning. I have two one-hour time blocks in my schedule each week to make sure I'm keeping up with the stack of books on my bedside table, and the list of titles, articles, and other information available digitally.

If you work for someone else, tell your boss about your desire to stay current with the industry and grow as an employee. Ask how much time they feel comfortable with for you to spend in this area. Many companies are open to the idea, and will allow you to use work time to learn. If you offer to share your findings with your boss or team you could even become a key resource for your department and company.

If your boss is not excited about you spending your time learning, do it on your own time. Dedicate an hour or two at night or on the weekends to seeking knowledge. You will further your career and become an indispensable asset to your company.

TAKE ADVANTAGE OF NATURAL DOWN TIMES

How can you incorporate learning into your commute? I love turning my car into a roaming university. For a while I was regularly buying or checking out audiobooks. Now I have an account on Audible.com, and get a new book every month. Whether you're using public transportation, walking, biking, or driving yourself, you can use the time you spend commuting to the office, to meetings, or even running errands to further your education. What other down time do you have? Consider ways you can keep a book or blog roll handy at the doctor's office or while waiting in line at the deli. I have a friend who listens to a book on tape while she's getting ready in the morning, and another who listens while she exercises. You might be surprised how much time you have that can be used to increase your knowledge base.

SCHEDULE TIME TO APPLY WHAT YOU'VE LEARNED

Gaining knowledge is a good thing, but it doesn't do much good unless you actively use it. Schedule time to apply the things you're learning in the various aspects of your job or business. After I attend a learning event or read a book, I schedule time the following week to review my notes, and tackle the ideas I received and put them into action. Information may be power, but application and action equals paychecks.

DON'T LET LEARNING OVERPOWER YOUR PRODUCTIVITY

It is possible to get so caught up in learning that you aren't accomplishing anything in your life or business. There are enough articles, teleseminars, live events, and courses available for you to spend all day every day in learning activities. Don't fall victim to this trap. While learning should be a lifelong pursuit, it should not be your *only* pursuit. Keep your learning time proportionate to the other areas of your life.

Always keep learning at the forefront of your endeavors. Invest in you. Be open to the knowledge of others and think about how collaborating can benefit your job, your company, and your industry as a whole. Make education a life-long pursuit that doesn't end the day you finish your formal degree or training. Seek to learn continually and then Make It Happen.

PLASTICITY IN ACTION

- Figure out your favorite way(s) to learn. Create routines around the outlets you enjoy most. Read at night before you go to bed, listen to podcasts and audio books on the subway during your commute, and decide how frequently you can afford to attend live events. Make a plan for whatever works best, and then schedule those activities in your calendar.
- Choose subjects outside of your profession and parenthood that interest you. If you need a place to start, my favorites are art, astronomy, nature and history.
- Find and subscribe to the trade publications in your industry, or put your favorite blogs in your RSS feed.

- Locate trade associations in your industry. Check out the resources they offer and look for events you can attend.
- Schedule time for learning into your week, but also keep good things to read and listen to close at hand for those extra or unexpected down times.

CHAPTER 12
PEOPLE-CENTRIC

"Earn your success based on service to others,
not at the expense of others."
—H. Jackson Brown Jr.

When we start the conversation about high performance, it can be easy to think about fattening bank accounts, promotions, media attention and more stereotypes that accompany success. Yet, I have learned over the years that my business and my life are only as strong as my relationships, and that in the end the money doesn't matter as much as the people do.

If you wanted to find me in high school, your best bet would have been to look in the debate room. To say I found my "home" in debate is an understatement. This girl loves to talk!

I enjoyed everything about it. Writing speeches, practicing, research, and writing briefs and cases. Then there was the competition aspect. I love competition!

I turned out to be good at it, too. Have you heard the school of thought that says if you do anything for two hours a day you can be among the best at it? I spent a lot of time working on my speaking skills and practicing with my partner in team debate. It paid off. I won many a trophy in high school, and debate paid for the first three years of my college education. I can't claim I was always the best, but I often won medals and trophies at competitions and I was certainly in the top ten in the state—I worked hard for that ranking.

My junior year of high school I was to be part of the "A" team for Mountain View High School. It was my partner Eric's senior year, and I worked especially hard to get him to state and ultimately nationals. We practiced a lot. I pored over evaluations from competitions, and practiced some more, even by myself. I'm pleased to say that we were the number one team and undefeated in the tournament that qualified us to go to nationals. Not too shabby for a junior!

That summer, while I prepared for my own senior year, I attended two debate camps, one in Michigan and one in my home state (Utah) with the debaters I knew and had competed against.

I'm not gonna lie—I felt like pretty hot stuff at debate camp. It didn't hurt that other students told me how awesome I was for my speaking awards and nationals qualifier. They expected a lot of me, and I worked hard to deliver. During our two-week in-state debate camp, we attended a symposium featuring the director, Dennis Edmunds, who was retiring. He gave a "last lecture" of sorts during which he shared life and success principles above and beyond debate tactics and strategies. He emphasized with passion the importance of the way we treat others. "I hope when people look at Michelle they don't just see a good debater," he said as he pointed directly at me. "I hope they see a nice person, too."

I'd like to believe I was a nice person before I got called out in front of everyone, but that experience pierced me and I haven't been the same since. Was I a nice person? His words from more than 15 years ago ring in my years on a regular basis. Am I a nice person now?

I knew then, as I know now, that no win or trophy means more than how I treat others. Our job title or accolades mean little if people look at us and first think, "Jerk."

High performers must be careful to maintain the proper balance between chasing dreams without stepping on others, and looking down on people when we have arrived. Once performance, status, or goals are reached, it can be easy to gloat or become pompous. As we talked about previously, a little PRIDE is necessary in the personal development game, but let me be clear—no award, no paycheck, and no achievement is more important than being kind.

Whether you're a stay-at-home parent or a CEO, I believe to my core that what Ty Bennett says is true: "We are in the people business."

You can't be selective about whom you treat with kindness. It's not okay to be nice to co-workers and family and rude to strangers. It's not okay to be nice to your boss and rude to the grocery store clerk who accidentally rings something up incorrectly. Self-mastery isn't just about how we act with the people closest to us—it's how we treat everyone.

I'm not going to spend too long on this subject, but if you're seeking the next level in your life or business, check your interactions with friends, family, co-workers, and even people you've never met.

My wise friend Monty once said, "Life is just a long test in interpersonal relationships." He couldn't be more right. Our character shows up in bold ways when we snap at someone on the street for bumping into us, or if we allow road rage to get the best of us.

Someone once posed a powerful question to me in asking, "What is it costing you to be right?"

Think about that for a minute. Have you ever had a relationship that eroded because you cared more about being right than preserving it?

Whom do you want to be? Do your interactions with others support high performance? High performers rise above demeaning behavior. They take the high road. They lead the way for others by proving that kindness matters.

I hate hearing adages like, "Nice girls don't get the corner office." And, "Nice guys finish last." Why do we perpetuate these notions? Personally, I'd rather be last than put someone else down to get there first.

If this sounds like an open invitation to be a doormat, it's not. You shouldn't allow people to treat you poorly. That being said, there is a positive way to respond without hurting the relationship. Carefully sharing your views and feelings when it's appropriate and without snapping or arguing will allow you to stand up for yourself in a way that doesn't demean the other person.

With introspection, humility, and care, many volatile relationships can be fixed. Start today with an open dialogue that sounds something like, "I know in the past we've communicated in a way that wasn't good for either of us. I'm sorry. I'd like to stop that today and move forward with a healthier way of communicating. From now on, I will show my respect for you through the way we talk."

Don't be surprised if, while fixing eroded relationships, you find you receive new levels of support in your goals and dreams. It's happened to me. I had a relationship with a family member that needed to change. It was hard, but with a sincere apology and a commitment to new ways (and then actually doing them), I found that person became my biggest supporter. I could not do what I do without them. Where before they were putting blocks in my way, they are now helping me remove them.

If there were a code of ethics and responsibility for how high performers treat others, I believe it would be this:

- High performers don't just understand the value of a person—they understand the value of *every* person.
- High performers don't seek success, fame, or fortune at the expense of another. They know people are of the highest value, and there is no better success than making a difference in the life of just one person.
- High performers are good listeners. They know that *all* people—friends, strangers, neighbors, children, retirees, coworkers, acquaintances, customers, and lovers—want to be heard and understood. They practice the timeless principle of the great Stephen Covey, "Seek first to understand, then to be understood."
- High performers put customers first and know there is greater success in approaching a sale from the customer's point of view. They value meeting someone's need over making a sale.
- High performers understand it's not about a transaction—it's about making customers for life.
- High performers provide value, even if the end result is no sale.
- High performers see friendship as a two-way street. They give more than they take and help others reach their goals.
- High performers believe and practice the Zig Ziegler principle that states, "You will get all you want in life if you help enough other people get what they want."
- High performers know love and marriage are important and fragile. They take romantic relationships seriously and take daily measures to strengthen them. They are fiercely protective of their companions and support them with passion.

- High performers know their knowledge can be used for the good of others. They are mentors, teachers, and influencers.
- High performers understand that their circle of influence goes beyond the home and office. They smile at strangers, help passers-by, and make a concerted effort to increase the happiness level of everyone they meet.
- High performers value every person regardless of station, class, or circumstances. They never belittle, demean, or put down anyone. They seek to equalize the playing field and understand the opportunities for all.
- High performers do not allow bullying of any kind. They don't bully others and they don't look away when they see someone being bullied. They notice such behavior taking place and they stop it.
- High performers compete to become their best selves regardless of the actions and progress of others.
- High performers use the Internet and social media to spread positivity and share their messages powerfully.

PEOPLE-CENTRIC IN ACTION

- Spend a day smiling at everyone you pass. Look into their eyes and send a positive glance their way. Try acknowledging people and see what it does for them (and you).
- Download the "Code of Ethics for High Performers" by getting the *Make It Happen Workbook* at speakmichelle.com/books. Post the code somewhere you'll see it on a regular basis.
- Ask yourself, "What is it costing me to be right?" Allow yourself to leave stubbornness behind you.
- Think about any relationships in your life that have been eroded by your poor behavior. Are there steps you can take, grudges you can let go of, or words you can say to mend them?

CHAPTER 13
POWER TEAM

"You are the average of the five people you spend the most time with."
—Jim Rohn

Do you believe the people you spend time with affect who you are and who you become?

I don't think it's an accident we were sent to a world full of people. I believe part of our purpose in life is learning a little (or a lot) about human interaction and interpersonal communication. Many of those lessons come from the people we're closest to and interact with most. That's why it's important to surround ourselves with inspiring individuals. It doesn't matter if you are an entrepreneur, a working professional, or a stay-at-home mom—everyone needs a power team.

We need our go-to people who support us, motivate us, check in on us, and cheer us on.

THE THREE LEVELS OF SUPPORT

Choosing your power team is just as important as choosing how to spend your time. You need the right people in the right place at the right time in your life. I like to think of the power team in terms of a pyramid with three levels. Each level serves its own purpose, and each is critical in its own way.

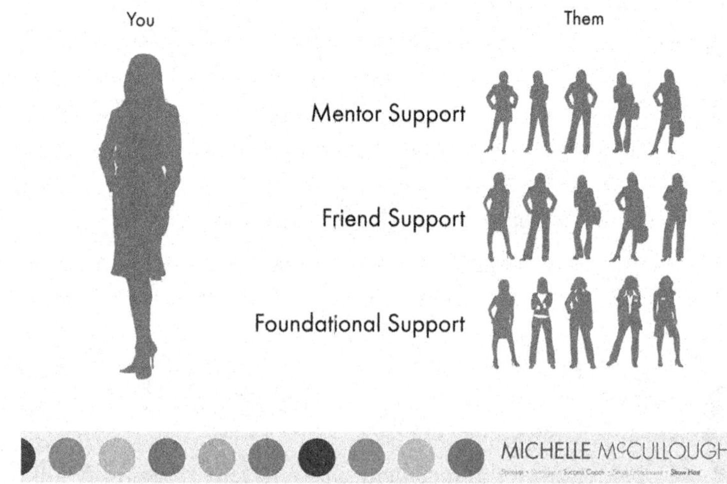

Odds are you already have people who support you on the various levels. As we discuss each one, think of who in your life fits in that category, and who else you could include to expand your power team and operate at your desired high performance level. You may even want to write down names as they come to you. And remember, just as you need people on your team, high performers should be part of other people's power teams as well.

1. Foundational Support

Every team needs a strong base, and your power team is no different. The foundational support level is comprised of people who assist you and can have responsibilities delegated to them. Since high performers know their strengths and delegate the rest, they rely on the people at the foundational support level to help them get things done.

Lower-Level Tasks

There are two types of tasks that are typically delegated. The first are the lower-level tasks. These are things that should be handled by an assistant, a contractor, or someone at a lower pay level. That doesn't mean the tasks, or the people doing them, are of lower value. Delegation is simply a way of dispersing tasks to the appropriate level of expertise.

I love Ken Blanchard's book *The One Minute Manager Meets the Monkey*. In it, Blanchard explains that "All monkeys must be handled at the lowest organizational level consistent with their welfare." This single principle has guided my professional life for the last 14 years.

When working for others, I got a lot of points for taking "monkeys" off my bosses' backs. I was a valued employee because I freed up their time to do what only they could do. I pushed to have every other task handed to me, and they appreciated me for it.

Hire and train the right employees, contractors, and vendors to help you do administrative activities so you can focus on your core strengths.

Skill-Based and Upper-Level Tasks

The second type of task that can be delegated involves things that are either above your level of expertise, or require skills you don't have. These are called skill-based or upper-level tasks.

For example, I have a client who is a graphic designer. After going through a delegation activity with her, I noticed she was spending one to two hours a week, sometimes more, on bookkeeping. As a creative person, she should spend most of her time creating art, graphics, and marketing materials. Instead, she was crunching numbers and tracking payments. Not only did she hate doing it, she really wasn't good at it.

Because she hated this task, she ended up dreading it every single week. Sometimes it got pushed into another week and then pushed into another week. By the time she got around to it she had to spend an entire afternoon or even a full day of bookkeeping and invoicing just so she could get paid. For her, bookkeeping was something she needed to delegate to someone else.

When I pointed this out, she said, "But Michelle, I can't afford it." So I asked her, "Well, how much do you make an hour?" She replied, "It depends on the project, but about $75 to $100 an hour." To that I said, "Okay, so for the $150 to $200 a week you are spending on bookkeeping, you could afford to hire a professional to do it for you." Light bulbs went on, and I think she may have done a dance on the spot. The point is, as an entrepreneur you do not have to do everything yourself!

Take a look at your current to-do list. Better yet, look at some completed lists or back lists. If something is not in your area of expertise, or if it is not something you really want to be doing, you should be delegating it to a professional who can do it better. Or, you might even consider finding an assistant (temporary or long-term) who can do it faster or for less money than it would cost you to do it.

I learned this lesson early on when I started my first business, a promotional products company. I would spend a lot of time putting stickers on catalogs, writing the addresses, and mailing them out, before I realized I could have a neighborhood teenager do those things for less cost. Delegating the tasks freed up my time so I could focus on marketing and getting new customers. What was even better was the fact that I had some happy neighbor kids who were getting paid to do something other than flip burgers. They liked the money, they were learning to work, and I had time for more important activities.

If you're an entrepreneur and could use additional help in this department, I dedicate two full chapters in my book *The Time Blueprint for Entrepreneurs* (available at Amazon.com) to the hows and whys of delegating.

If you're not an entrepreneur, get creative about the ways you can utilize others' strengths and resources to get the "monkeys" off your back and build the foundational level of your power team.

2. Core Friend Support

The middle level of the support team is for our friends and family members. These people are our cheerleaders—sometimes literally. They are the ones who are sitting on the front row at our events, by our side during key moments in life, and celebrating every victory with us. They also have their arms around us when we lose. We can trust and rely on them.

My friends and family are my rock. They are the ones I turn to when things get tough. They are the shoulders I cry on for support when I fail. While the other two levels of support can be appropriately one-sided (because you are making monetary investments and getting a service in return), the friend level only works if it is mutually beneficial.

At times you may at times have greater needs than your friend, and vice versa. Trust, communication, support, and love need to be given and received on both sides. I feel I have been abundantly blessed in this category. I have great girlfriends who get me through my days and weeks. I have great business friendships in which we support each other in the ups and downs of professional life. I have family members I know are always there for me, and I would do anything for them. I honestly couldn't do what I do without good friends.

Do you have people like this in your life? Are you that type of person for others? Typically, this level is where people naturally have the most support. However, if you find yourself lacking in this category, I have a couple of suggestions to help you build a stronger power team of friends.

- **Connect with like-minded individuals.** Networking events and social groups are a great way to seek out like-minded individuals. There are so many options! Professionally, consider chambers of commerce and other groups with potential to strengthen your business associations and friendships. Personally, consider sports teams, clubs, and organizations surrounding interests or hobbies you enjoy.
- **Find online groups via social media.** If you do a quick search through Facebook, Google+, or LinkedIn, you'll find groups focused on almost any topic, interest, and industry. Although these types of relationships obviously can't compare to live, one-on-one interaction, you can find like-minded individuals all across the world. Join in the conversation and glean what you can from their wisdom and experiences. Where appropriate, reach out to connect with individuals on a more direct level.
- **Consider what kind of friend you are in return.** With some honesty and transparency, some of my clients have discovered the reason they are weak at this power team level is that they haven't been supportive of others. This has left them with a social void in their life. It's never too late to repair what might seem broken, or make connections with new people.

One thing to note about this level is that the people come and go as time goes on. I've noticed in my life how friends change as my lifestyle, circumstances, and even location change. With a handful of exceptions, the friends I had in junior high school are not the friends I have now, at least not the ones I keep in contact with regularly. I assume that's the case for you as well, and that is certainly the case in life and business. The good news is, as our opportunities grow and change, people enter exactly when we need them.

As you change careers or grow from mediocre to high performer, you may find there are some people who don't want to reach the summit with you. That's okay. Take the time to bring along those who want to grow with you, and wish the best to those who don't.

Spend time with people who love you, who support you, and who care about your well-being. If you're in a relationship that is draining or unhealthy, make plans to decrease the time you spend with them and increase the time you spend with the people who are helping you move forward. When done with a healthy attitude and a loving heart we can make decisions that are right for us.

3. Mentor Support

Mentor or coach support is the top level of the support team. I picture mentors and coaches as being above me. In other words, they are the people who know what I want to know, and they have blazed a trail for me to follow. I want and need their support to help me get to my destination faster.

Mentors come in many forms. They can be a friends with knowledge or skill sets you want to learn. They can be business associates who teach and train you. Whatever form they take on, they are knowledge givers, coaches, and consultants.

I worked at a television station while I was in college. My boss was a nice, smart man who to this day is one of the most organized and polished people I know. He even had a specific system for ironing his shirts so the creases would be just so. He never had a hair on his head out of place, and all of his folder tabs faced in one direction.

I remember being surprised when he told me one day that he had hired a life coach. Honestly, I had to try really hard not to laugh out loud. I couldn't believe Mr. Perfection needed help achieving more in his life. I critically thought, "If you can't figure out how to handle your own life, you might have bigger problems."

The irony is that I'm a coach now. I get it. Even though I coach clients across the country and in various parts of the world, I still pay coaches to help keep me in my A-game. I find people with a skill or expertise I want to acquire and then I learn from them. Coaches help me "get there faster" in my life and business, and I see my coaches as prime examples of the mentor support that's helped me become a high performer.

Though I have paid people to coach me, I have also used the help of free mentors, mastermind groups, and accountability partners, all of whom I consider to be important parts of my power team.

The people you spend your time with can impact your projects and dreams in big ways. They can cheer you on, support you, and help you grow, but they can also discourage and distract you with their "let's be realistic" comments. Be careful about those you include on your power team, and the time and energy investment you make in people who are raining on your parade.

I feel very blessed to have amazing people in my life at every level. I couldn't accomplish what I do without employees, mentors, friends, and family members who show up in powerful ways to help me on my journey as a high performer.

Take some time to tend your own relationships and help your power team understand what their support, at any level, means to you! Quality time and gratitude build strong relationships. Multiple deposits into the relationship bank (even for people on your foundational level, and even if you're paying them for the work they do) are required to keep those bonds strong. Think through your three levels of support: what practices can you put into place that will help you cultivate and grow healthy relationships?

Many of our practices can be broken down into daily, weekly, and monthly tasks. Daily tasks are things such as phone calls, emails, and messages via social media. Weekly tasks require more time. For example, I like to sit down and write physical letters each week. In this day and age, the art of good old-fashioned snail mail is all but forgotten. I love getting thank you cards and notes from friends. I appreciate the extra effort (finding my physical address, handwriting something, getting a stamp, and getting it to the mail box is a lot of work), and it's fun to get something in the mail that isn't a bill or advertisement. Likewise, people will appreciate the effort you put forth in this regard. Another weekly task that is helpful (if you have employees) is scheduling one-on-one check-in meetings. These don't have to be long, but they can be a great way to keep the lines of communication open while discussing tasks and areas of growth and improvement. For monthly tasks, decide how many networking events you will attend each month, and how you'll connect with a mentor or accountability partner. Also, decide how and when you'll get together for social events with core friends.

A NOTE ON NAYSAYERS

"How do I deal with people who just don't get it?" – This is a common question from my coaching clients. They share story after story of friends, loved ones, and even acquaintances telling them how CRAZY they are for working on a big goal. Has this ever happened to you? Whether it's someone close, or someone who should be minding their own business, there are a number of ways to respond (or freak out). Yet three guiding principles should be remembered when dealing with even the most "well meaning" of naysayers.

1. Always be kind, it's hard to get the support that you need, if you meet their judgment-filled for-your-own-good comments. It's not worth the fight. When tensions escalate, use the fall back, "Thank you for your feedback," and change the subject.
2. Remember, the fastest way to quiet naysayers is results. It may not work in all instances, but take action, get some traction under your big goal or project and you may find that they show up to rally and support you, know that they know you are fully committed.
3. Own that you may need to have a better, more enrolling conversation with the naysayer. Tell them exactly how they CAN support you, but do it in a way that they will listen. The next chapter, Persuasion, has a blueprint for having important conversations of support with every level in your support structure.

A NOTE ON FAMILY

The most critical part of my power team is my family—my husband and kids, even my mom, brothers, sisters, aunts, uncles, and cousins. I involve them in my goals and dreams and bring them along as best I can for the ride. I place them in the core friend category. They are people I love who cheer me on and see me through.

Because they are an essential and fulfilling part of my life, I make time for them every day and every week. I've put practices in place to ensure we have a deep connection. Date night with my husband happens once a week—97% of the time. I never want my marriage to suffer because I'm too busy to make it a priority. We send text messages to each other throughout the day and we take some time each night to connect, read together, and sit in the same room (even if we're both working on laptops for some of that time). We sit down every Monday to review our schedules for the week and get our date night on the calendar.

I also schedule time with my kids. Each day I carve out "mom time" during which we go to a park or the city rec center, or just hang out at home and play whatever game they're currently drawn to (even if it means I'm playing Go Fish for the umpteenth time). I also go on individual dates with my kids so I can build a one-on-one relationship with them. I like to hear their stories, and I've found they are different kids when they aren't competing for attention. Nurturing them as part of my power team is really important.

Some people have criticized me for having to "schedule" time with my family. While I've been accused of being too rigid in this category, I stand by my decision. I want my family to feel as important as any speaking engagement or a coaching call. I want them to know I care about them enough to make time for them.

My life can get incredibly busy. Between my family and work, it can be easy to put family and friends on the back burner. I justify it sometimes by saying, "They know things are busy. I'll reconnect when things slow down." But I need those relationships and those connections as much as they do. Getting such commitments on a calendar allows me to not just have good intentions in this area, but to actually Make It Happen.

POWER TEAM IN ACTION

- In your *Make It Happen Notebook*, write down the individuals who support you in each of the three levels: Foundational, Core Friend, and Mentor. Note levels where you feel incomplete, and make a special point to seek out individuals who can help you.
- Think about how you can help and support others with their goals. Where do you fit on the power team of your friends, co-workers and family? How can you be a better cheerleader and in what ways are you a great foundational support or mentor in your areas of proficiency?

- Send thank you notes and express verbal gratitude to those who support you in your dreams.
- Take time to tend relationships online as well as offline. Schedule lunch dates with friends and mentors, meet people in their home or office, etc.
- Research networking groups, clubs, and organizations you want to visit to see if they fit your life and goals.
- Read the next chapter on Persuasion so you can learn how to navigate important conversations to get the support you want.

CHAPTER 14
PERSUASION

"Don't raise your voice, improve your argument."
—Desmond Tutu

Bless my patient husband's heart. Living with a visionary like me can be a real trial. I constantly have ideas. Lots of ideas. I have ideas about businesses I want to start, trips I want to take, projects I'm ready to begin, activities to do with the kids, and new parenting tips I want to try. Many of my ideas require his help or support, but since I don't always take action on every idea, he listens to me talk and philosophize and then patiently waits for me to narrow them down before he involves himself. It's a lesson he's learned over time.

WHAT IS THE DIFFERENCE BETWEEN SIMPLY ASKING FOR HELP AND ENROLLMENT?

Enrollment is a conversation in which you share your vision with another person, discuss the desired outcome, and then agree on a course of action.

Over the years I've also learned a few things, including the difference between sharing my ideas and dreams and actually enrolling people in them. Persuasion is powerful, but it can often turn into manipulation if we're not careful. On the other end of the spectrum, sometimes we think we are enrolling people, when in actuality we aren't even clearly stating our needs. Many high performers are good communicators by nature, but if it's not a skill you have, it's definitely one you can master with practice.

I had to learn this the hard way. I hit bumps on my road to fine tuning this craft. For example, I produce events for entrepreneurs, and for years Startup Princess held an annual conference every fall. The second year I was involved I remember having an especially busy week before the date of the conference. I thought I was enlisting the help of my husband each time I made a statement such as, "There's so much to do." or "I don't know how I'm going to get all of this done." My husband didn't see what I was really saying was, "Will you help me, please?"

I was frustrated that he wasn't getting it, and I continued on this way until I finally snapped. In a moment of anger I barked at him, "Don't you remember I have a big event this week?" Still, he didn't interpret this as meaning, "Will you please help me?" Instead, he calmly responded, "Yes, I do. Did you need my help? You seemed organized and like you had everything under control."

I'm ashamed to say that this experience eroded a little of my most important relationship, and it was no one's fault but my own. I hadn't been expressing my needs clearly, yet I was upset when my husband didn't read my mind and come to my rescue. It was a communications breakdown on my part.

Has something like this ever happened to you? Stop expecting the people in your life to have a crystal ball. If you want help, support, or encouragement, ask for it!

When it comes to high performance and goal achievement, we can all do better at enrolling people in our vision. Giving orders, dictating assignments, or yelling commands won't entice people to willingly support your mission. I've found the most effective form of persuasion is enrollment.

HOW DOES ENROLLMENT WORK?

Lucky for you, I've done the dirty work on what works and what doesn't when it comes to enrollment. After a lot of trial and error, I've fine-tuned a simple formula for negotiating and creating a solid win-win agreement you can use to get the results you want.

As I lay out the steps, consider how enrollment can work in relationships with your spouse, boss, employees, friends, kids, family, and others. The words and the approach may be different, but the general idea will be the same.

First, share the vision. Explain your goal and tell them why it's important to you. Help them understand the passion driving you to chase this dream and what it will mean to you when you achieve it. Passion is contagious.

Second, commit to the goal. You may even want to say the words, "I've thought this out." This one has been especially helpful in my relationships since ideas flow out of my mouth freely. I want people I'm talking with to know I've sifted through other ideas, and I'm committed to this one. In some cases you have to acknowledge that you realize past goals have flopped, but you're committed this time.

Third, explain the plan and outline the specific support you need to accomplish your goal or project. What roles do other people play in this plan? Do you simply need support and encouragement, or are there specific action items you will need to assign someone?

This is where a lot of the conversation will take place because it's not just about getting what you want. There could be circumstances you haven't considered or valid questions or concerns raised by your counterpart. Be open to adjusting the plan in favor of creating a mutually beneficial situation.

Once you feel you're on the same page, the fourth and most important step is asking what I call a question of support. It's essentially the handshake of the conversation and can be something as simple as, "Can I get your support in this project?" One of my favorite questions is, "Under what circumstances could I get your support on this?" (Sometimes that question slips into Step Three.)

Here's an example of how I should have approached my husband for help during event week.

- Step 1: "Hi Honey. You've probably seen on the calendar that our big event is coming up next week. I'm feeling overwhelmed by it all. This event is important to our business. We have more than 150 women coming from all across the country, and I really want everything to run smoothly so we can make a good impression."
- Step 2: "I know in the past I've left a lot of things to the last minute, and I'm committed to working over the next couple of days so I'm not crazy two days before the event."
- Step 3: "There are a lot of ways I could use your help accomplishing this. I'm going to need some extra help with the baby this week and I'd also really appreciate it if you could take care of dinner. If you have some extra time at

night, I could use your help putting together packets and typing name tags."

- Step 4: "What things would you be willing to help me do?"

Being clear and specific is much more effective in persuading people to enlist in your cause. This is especially true if your previous tactic has been snapping at people when they don't read your mind. (Ahem.)

Consider how this could work if you're asking a friend or loved one to help you accomplish a goal. I'm going to show you one more (hypothetical) example.

- Step 1: "Hi Friend. This year, my goal is to lose 40 pounds. I really want to be healthier, and I feel like losing the weight will help me feel better about myself and allow me to keep up with my family."

  (She, of course, congratulates me and says some encouraging words.)
- Step 2: "The holidays were a bust to my routine and I got out of the habit of exercise. Starting now I'm going to give up soda and go to the gym five times a week. I also talked to my doctor and she recommended the right calorie intake for my body and goals, so I'm going to track my food every day."

  (She says additional encouraging things like, "Awesome! You've got this!"
- Step 3: "I know I've trained you and all of my other friends to bring me a treat every time you bake, so I'm going to need to respectfully decline them so I'm not tempted. I'd also love to check in with you once a week for a little accountability."

  (She's nodding at this point, and patting me on the back. Hypothetically, of course.)
- Step 4: "Could you help me with those two things?"

Works like a charm.

This process is especially powerful when you delegate a task to an employee or anyone who may be helping you with something. Here's an outline of an enrolling conversation in a work environment.

- Step 1: "Hi Sandy, we're getting ready for a big product launch and we're super excited. The initial buzz has been awesome and I can't wait to see the response. This product is really going to help."
- Step 2: "Our goal is to have a huge opening week by taking preorders three weeks in advance. Our print and television advertising campaign is in full swing, and our social media campaign starts heavily next week."
- Step 3: "We're asking the marketing department to implement a specific marketing strategy. As the social media intern, I'd like you to work closely with Adam to make sure we keep up with our posting and engagement schedule as outlined in the strategy. The timing is critical for maximum viewership, likes, and sharing."
- Step 4: "Are you on board with us to complete this social media strategy? Do you have any other priorities on your plate we might need to reassign in order for this to come to the front burner?"

The whole conversation took sixty seconds, but the vision was presented, the tasks explained, and a commitment question was put in place to make sure it was all understood.

Enrollment works for every relationship. I can even use it to persuade my small children to get on board with my unpredictable speaking schedule. Some might say they're too small to understand, but even when they were toddlers who spoke in three- word sentences,

ENROLLMENT - FORMAT FOR SUCCESS

- The Dream - I have been thinking that I want to...
- The Commitment - This is something I've been thinking about for a long time.
- The Plan - Some things that need to be done in order to make this happen...
- The Question of Support - Do I have your support? Are you on board? Can you help me with...?

I took time to have a conversation and talk them through each step. The pattern of good communication can be learned early, and I want them to learn it from me. I also want them to know I'm involving them instead of working around them.

Simple kid conversations can sound like this. "Hi, doll baby. I'm going on a plane this week to help a group of women. I'm going to be gone for a few days, but when I get back I'm taking a couple of days off and we're going to the park and making cookies. Can you hug me before I go?"

Sometimes, these conversations happen as a result of a frustration expressed by your counterpart. It's a sign that enrollment is happening a little late, but better late than never.

While driving my then six-year-old son to a friend's house one afternoon so I could conduct a coaching call, he said in an exasperated tone, "I'm sick of your meetings and Startup Princess." After I got over the thought, "He knows the name of my business?" I said, "Hey, buddy. Do you know why mommy works?" He shook his head a little bit, and I continued, "I work to help other people who have a hard time in their business. I help them and give them tools so they aren't worried or stressed. I also work to help our family pay the bills and so we can do fun things. Do you like to go to Disneyland?" He perked up and smiled at me. "Dad works really hard to pay for our house and cars and food. My meetings help us pay for soccer and t-ball and so we can go on fun trips. Can you support me in my job so we can do fun things?"

The next day my son said to me, "Mom, do you need to work today? I'll be really quiet. I want to go to Disneyland."

Success!

Everyone wants to know how something is going to affect them, and when my kids understand why I do what I do, they don't cry as much at the door when I leave.

This system isn't foolproof and you shouldn't discount the exasperated outbursts from people close to you. It's easy for me to jump into an enrolling conversation, but I also need to hear the feedback. In the previous example I stepped up the presence with my son so he could reconnect with me. The explanation is good, the enrollment is good, but the best persuasion in getting the people you care about on board with your dreams is making sure you aren't persuading them at the expense of the relationship. They want to make sure they are still important, even if your clients/goals/projects are important, too.

The best persuasion technique is quality time. When quantity is low, quality needs to be especially high. Spend time in good conversation without digital distractions with those you love. When they know they are first, they will support you with your goal and as you work to Make It Happen.

PERSUASION IN ACTION

- Replay some past conversations and experiences in your head or write them on paper. How could you have approached someone differently to bring about better results?
- Get clear on your vision before you start an enrollment conversation. Take time to think through the details and the conversation before it happens. You'll feel more confident and prepared.
- Don't be afraid to apologize for past actions. If there are some trust issues that need to be repaired, or broken agreements that need to be mended, a simple apology goes a long way and helps you through the persuasion process. Consider apologizing first and letting that sink in for a day or two before you try to enroll them in what's next.
- If you're feeling uncomfortable with this direct approach (because you've been good at skirting around things in the past) practice in the mirror a few times. Intonation and facial expressions are just as important as the actual words.

CHAPTER 15
PRIDE

"Believe in yourself! Have faith in your abilities! Without a humble but reasonable confidence in your own powers you cannot be successful or happy."

—Norman Vincent Peale

Pride sometimes gets a bad rap, and I think it's because people often use it to mean arrogance. I believe arrogance is a repulsive quality that's rooted in a belief that one person is better than another person. On the other hand, I see pride as being a good thing. I use it to mean confidence and satisfaction in a job well done. From that perspective, pride is something everyone who wants to be a high performer needs.

High performers are confident in their abilities. They take pride in themselves, and pride in their work. They are quick to own their mission, and they show up powerfully to complete that mission. They understand their worth, and know that other people's achievements don't diminish their own, because each individual is responsible for his own success.

At one point in my career I worked at a large software company. I was on the inside sales floor with about seventy other employees. Our paychecks were performance based, which meant they depended entirely on how many deals we closed and contracts we renewed in relation to our quota. A scenario like that can create quite a sense of competition among coworkers—especially when results and progress are shared publicly.

My first year on the floor, one co-worker hit 120% of his quota in six months—an impressive feat. I watched him carefully, and noticed he always carried himself with a confident strut when he walked around the office. He never bragged or sought attention for his achievements. While it was obvious he took pride in them, he never used them to demean anyone else. To this day, I see him as a prime example of confidence, not arrogance.

Remember Richard, the helpful employee from the retail store I frequent? Richard is another prime example of a high performer who takes pride in his work. A high performer doesn't care what the job is, but only how well he completes it. He knows the greatest way to build character and confidence is to take ownership of a job, even if he works for someone else. After all, it seems like a waste to spend eight hours, and often more, on something you don't take pride in.

Confidence is the root of success, happiness, and fulfillment. Yet, there seems to be a lack of depth in this department. Too many people measure their worth by what everyone around them is doing. High performers don't fall into this trap. They are self-reliant and recognize that confidence is a practice, not a destination. It's something to be worked at, not an award that is received once and never spoken of again.

I have found that, without exception, every time I seek new levels in my life or my business, I'm faced with a difficult trial that challenges my confidence. I think that's true for everyone. The more we grow, the more we have our conviction tested.

Again, like failures or setbacks, these challenges are normal, and are not signs you should stop, or that you aren't destined for high performance status. David Neagle accurately says, "New level, new devil." It's in the challenge that we stretch and learn and qualify ourselves for greater things. So don't let that devil get you down or convince you that you can't Make It Happen.

PRIDE IN ACTION

- Set some achievable goals and work towards them. Review the section on Goal Gradation in the Planning chapter. Some of us have been breaking commitments and goals to ourselves for years, and we need to repair and rebuild trust in ourselves so we can eliminate our "I'm a failure" mentality.
- Make a list of all your good qualities and traits. Be sure to include your talents, skills, and abilities. This list is for your eyes only, so there's no need to hold back. If your list is short because you easily talk yourself out of the things you're good at, then ask five people who know you well to send you three words that best describe your positive qualities. It can be very enlightening.
- Consider how you currently approach your job or business and ask yourself if you're giving your very best effort. If you're not, determine what you can do to take pride in the job you were given.
- Look into creating an Ideal LifeVision with Ann Webb (We talk about this more in the chapter on Possibility) to get crystal clear

on what you want in all areas of your life. Ann's powerful tool helps you find your vision, but more importantly, it teaches you the power and effect your voice has on achieving your dreams. I'm a huge advocate of Ideal LifeVision. It has helped me reach countless goals, and has removed the frequent and degrading negative thoughts that were polluting my mind and eroding my self-worth.

- Create a confidence journal. Similar to a gratitude or joy journal, a confidence journal is where you record five things you're proud of yourself for doing that day.
- Take the "Mirror Exercise Challenge" in the *Make It Happen Workbook*.
- Read *The Big Leap* by Gay Hendricks, then send me an email and we can have a virtual book club.
- Find ways to challenge yourself and make personal development a lifelong pursuit.

CHAPTER 16
PHYSICAL HEALTH

"Physical fitness is not only one of the most important keys to a healthy body, it is the basis of dynamic and creative intellectual activity."

—John F. Kennedy

People who say, "Nothing tastes as good as thin feels," haven't tasted the things I have. Food and I are special friends. As an amateur foodie, I've eaten amazing things from all over the world. I love everything from fine foods to the cheese that comes in a can.

I didn't think my health had anything to do with my success until I was thirty-one. I had never really been active or athletic. I was in debate and drama in high school, and even though some of my friends found time to be on sports teams as well, it wasn't a priority for me. I spent most of my life convincing myself I was "fat and happy" and okay just the way I was. In a very real sense I was okay, but I was *only* "okay."

Then, in the spring of 2010, just after the birth of my second child, things changed for me. I had lost my "baby weight," but I had been pretty heavy before that. Some of my closest friends had started running and were losing weight like crazy. After months of watching them post their results on blogs and social media, I finally told myself, "If they can do it, I can do it."

You know how they always tell you to consult your physician before you begin an exercise program? Well, I did that. (For the record, she told me I was one of only a handful of her patients who actually followed that advice.) It was well worth it, as she recommended the right calorie intake for my body and goals, and told me to exercise at least 30 minutes a day, 3–5 days a week. The next thing I knew, I had a gym membership—and I was actually using it! I started going to the gym 4–6 days a week.

It didn't take long before the weight started coming off, and the more that came off, the more motivation I had to go to the gym. But it wasn't just about the weight loss—I loved the compliments I got. I loved people telling me how great I looked, and patting me on the back for working hard. After all, I *was* working hard, and it was nice to hear other people acknowledge that. But what surprised me was how many times people asked, "So what are you doing? What program?" My response was always the same: "Turns out diet and exercise works." I was surprised again when they would disappointedly reply, "Oh. Sad."

We're all looking for a quick fix. We all want it to be easy. We want to eat what we want and look like models at the same time, but unless you're genetically built that way, it's not going to happen.

After I dropped forty pounds, I realized my diet and exercise journey had taught me a very powerful principle: my body is the vehicle for my dreams. I have big dreams and big goals, and I need energy to accomplish them. It's not just about the energy to work, it's about the mental fortitude to handle the ups and downs of life. It's about having the vitality I need to be a rockstar mom and a rockstar entrepreneur at the same time. I still haven't reached my ideal weight, but I am making progress towards health being a lifestyle and not a limited-time diet, and that is bringing me closer to reaching my dreams and goals.

If your body is the vehicle to your dreams, are you fueling it well?

Before I lost weight, I didn't realize how much I was hiding behind my body and using it as an excuse to keep me from chasing my true goal of booking speaking engagements across the country. Now, I am more confident at networking events and in front of crowds, which makes me a stronger public speaker, trainer, and businesswoman.

For high performers, it's not just about weight loss, it's about optimum health. You may be at a place in your life when your weight is right for you and your circumstances. If that's the case, congratulations, but don't skip this chapter. High performance is not about a number on the scale, it's about vitality and confidence in your physical being. Whatever your number, remember that your weight doesn't define you, your contribution to the world does. Ask yourself on a regular basis, "Am I at my optimum health?" If the answer is no, correct the issue. Do you need more sleep? Do you need to adjust your food intake? Will exercise give you your needed endorphins?

What could you do if you were in better health? I'm certainly not a doctor, and you should consult yours if you're making changes to your health or exercise program, but I'm going to share a few things I've learned about making health a priority. I recognize that nothing I'm sharing here is new or innovative in the health and wellness arena, but sometimes we seek complicated or radical solutions, when the answers really lie in the simple tried and true steps that have always been in front of us.

1. **Find something you enjoy.** Try different types of exercise until you find a few you like. When I began working out, I was a Zumba junkie. In fact, I attribute the first twenty pounds I released to fast-paced dancing and the sweating that goes with it. After a while, I tired of it and wanted to try other things. I know a lot of people love running, and try as I might, I'm still not one of them. (Although I recently ran a half marathon—a plan I would have given up on if it weren't for the fact I announced I was doing it.) Don't feel bad if you don't subscribe to the same exercise programs as everyone else. You're the one who has to like it day after day, so find something that's right for you.
2. **Schedule exercise into your day.** If you want to make exercise a priority, you need to put it on your calendar. If you have to get up early before work, or go at different times each day because of a varying schedule, you'll set yourself up to succeed when you schedule a specific time. If you simply tell yourself you'll exercise when you have some free time, it will rarely if ever happen. Take it off your to-do list and put it on your daily events calendar.
3. **Drink enough water.** Again, consult your physician about the right amount of water intake for your body. I love a refreshing cold glass of water, but through listening to Deepak Chopra's *Boundless Energy* I learned the value of warm water throughout the day. Chopra shares the general health and digestive benefits of warm water to increase your energy and productivity. I listened to that book more than ten years ago, and it has made a big difference.
4. **Eat your fruits and vegetables.** When I go to the grocery store, I make sure to choose at least ten different fruits and veggies to keep on hand so I have lots of variety when I'm hungry. When I get home, I wash, cut, and package them all to create grab-and-go servings. That way, when a craving hits, I have healthy

options at my fingertips. Elizabeth Anderson, a former Mrs. Utah who is a health and wellness coach, often reminds me that proper nutrition is about eighty percent of the health and weight loss battle.

5. **Don't skip breakfast.** That's not an old wives tale—eating a healthy breakfast goes a long way to starting your day off right. Not only does it kickstart your metabolism and keep your body from panicking and holding on to fat as it wonders when the next meal is coming, but it gives you the energy you need to think and function properly.
6. **Keep a healthy mindset.** Exercise and eating healthy are just as much mental games as they are physical. I have many emotions connected to food and exercise, and many scripts I've been reading from for almost three decades. Those are hard to reprogram. Obtaining the mindset of a healthy and vibrant body is just as important as doing the work it takes to actually be healthy. If you need help working through some of your misperceptions, get help. A good personal trainer or transformational coach can help you put together a game plan for getting your brain on board with your new body changes.
7. **Take a daily multivitamin.** Everyone says you're supposed to take a multivitamin, but I tried a lot of different kinds and never felt a difference. Then a friend of mine practically dared me to try Lifelong Vitality by doTERRA for 30 days. Prior to taking Lifelong Vitality, a typical day included putting my 18-month-old down for a nap, turning on a show for my three-year-old (who, heaven help me, had decided he was done with naps long ago), and squeezing in a quick 30-minute power nap for myself. It wasn't a luxury, it was an almost daily necessity. A month into taking Lifelong Vitality, I realized I hadn't taken a single nap

since I started, and even without a nap, I had noticeably more energy and was more productive. I could have said these results were a fluke, or attributed them to other factors, but a few months later I gave my month's supply of Lifelong Vitality to a friend to try. Within a week I was back to being lethargic and needing regular naps. Lifelong Vitality is now an important part of my health regimen. There are a lot of multivitamin options out there, and they certainly aren't all created equal. Your doctor can help you select one that's right for you.

8. **Get enough sleep.** No book can tell you exactly how many hours of sleep you need each night to operate as a high performer. Every person is different. I have a friend who survives, functions, and is at his optimum health when he gets only five or six hours of sleep per night. He can do this night after night. I can do that for one night, but not on a regular basis. For a time, I could survive on six hours of sleep. It wasn't until I was in a health challenge with some friends with the overall objective of health (we were given a score based on healthy eating, exercise, water intake, and sleep) that I realized I needed seven hours of sleep every night, and often more! On the challenge we were required to sleep at least seven hours each night or there was a penalty in our score. I have never felt better, and now I aim for eight hours of sleep each night. As a work-at-home mom, I often do the bulk of my day's work when my kids are asleep. I get carried away from time to time and stay up too late. Sadly, my kids don't get the memo to sleep in. I've learned that increasing my sleep at night increases my energy, productivity, and my mental clarity during the day. When you choose to sacrifice sleep, you also choose to sacrifice your health and the quality of your work. If you spend most of your day tired (or you use artificial stimulants to keep you going through the day) try to get one or

two hours more of sleep on a regular basis and see if that helps your high performance.

I'm not the only one who has discovered the business benefits of healthy living. Corporations large and small have recognized that healthy employees take fewer sick days, contribute to reduced insurance rates, and are generally happier. As a result, more and more businesses are including gyms in their offices, or providing free or reduced-cost gym memberships for their employees. They are incorporating health and wellness challenges and encouraging proper nutrition. If your company doesn't currently offer these programs, lead the charge by talking to your human resources department. If you work alone, it might be harder to make exercise part of your normal routine. Try teaming up with friends or other entrepreneurs to make healthy living a habit. It will be well worth it for the increase in energy, mental fortitude, and performance.

A big key to maintaining a healthy lifestyle is creating sustainable habits. My friend KrisTina is deeply motivated in her health goals and I admire her dedication. After the birth of her first baby, she wanted to shed some baby weight plus a bit more. She made exercise a priority almost every day, and created an eating plan that motivated her. That plan included no sugar, sweets, dessert, or treats. For her, it worked.

On the other hand, I turn into a crazy person if I completely deny myself. I learned that the hard way. I used to think the only way to maintain a healthy lifestyle was to give up the things I loved. This made me discouraged, frustrated, and obsessive about chocolate chip cookies to the point where I'd throw my "plan" out the window and eat a dozen cookies in one sitting. Not exactly a healthy mindset.

I've since learned the value of moderation and discovered that when I allow myself one cookie, and keep track of it in my food journal, it's easier to make healthy choices and eat sensibly for the rest of the day.

So which is better? Is it better to take the KrisTina approach and go cold turkey, or the moderation approach and allow yourself the things you want, but in smaller quantities? That all depends on what works for you. This principle applies in most aspects of exercise and nutrition. Make healthy choices, but make choices that you can sustain, as opposed to those that will lead to yo-yo dieting.

Have you seen the documentary *Fat, Sick and Nearly Dead*? It is a very interesting commentary on the science of juicing and the importance of eating vegetables. What I like most about the film is the before and after examples Joe Cross shared. He talks about how his business improved because he had increased energy, was more dynamic in his relationships with board members and staff, and had more mental clarity to address issues and projects.

In my journey of health, I've found the same to be true for me. I'll bet if you were to look at the high performers in your life, you'd find it to be true for them, too. They crave health and energy and it's just as important as meeting sales quotas and landing a big new client. In fact, it's the fuel to be able to perform at work. So while some of you don't need the weight benefits of exercise and proper nutrition, you could likely still benefit from the clarity of mind and energy that comes from taking care of your body.

PHYSICAL HEALTH IN ACTION

- Take a minute to write down some of your thoughts about actions you can take to improve your health. Do you need an exercise or eating plan? Do you need the support of a trainer or coach? Do you need to work on scheduling exercise into your day? Write some notes in your *Make It Happen Notebook,* and get out your calendar and schedule your exercise for the week.

- Consult a doctor or medical health professional on an exercise and eating program that is appropriate for your current circumstances, body type, and health goals.
- Get clear on your "why" for your physical health goals. What will optimum health do for your energy? How will it help you personally and professionally? Write it down, read it on a regular basis, and refer to it when your motivation is low. Some people are highly motivated by an upcoming event (like a class reunion or media opportunity), others are motivated by health challenges, and some people need a mix of both. My best motivation is my why. When I'm rooted in the big picture I make healthy eating choices and get back on track with my exercise schedule.
- If you've been telling yourself some harsh words about your body, your energy or your health, reframe them to be positive comments. Get professional help if you find yourself struggling with some of the mental challenges associated with optimum health.
- If you don't have one already, create a goal for your water intake. Do you need the right drinkware to motivate you? What reminders can you put in place to help you reach your goal?
- Sometimes the key to success is a good tracking system. Track your food intake, minutes spent exercising, etc. I have friends who track how many miles they run each day for an impressive running total at the end of the year. I track my calories based on the guidelines by my doctor—the tracking itself helps me make better choices. My mom put a small calendar on her fridge and simply puts a smiley face on the days she exercises. It makes her smile to see all the happy faces looking at her for a job well done.

CHAPTER 17
PLAY

"It is a happy talent to know how to play."
—Ralph Waldo Emerson

I had a client who was consistently working 60 and 70-hour weeks. Even with two assistants, the nature of her job simply meant there was always a lot to be done. When she wasn't working, she devoted every spare minute she had to her family. Somewhere along the way, she realized there was never any time to do the things she once enjoyed, like make art or participate in other creative outlets. She had essentially sacrificed all her own hobbies and the things she liked doing in favor of the job and her family.

While being a good employee, parent, and spouse are admirable, sacrificing yourself is not a positive high performance practice.

High performers can only operate at their high when their whole being is in alignment. If you spend month after month suppressing the things that make you the happiest because you feel like "Sacrifice" needs to be your middle name, then you're missing the point. Time and space for play will help you develop into the whole being you were meant to be.

I encouraged this particular client to take one small step a week to get her creative wheels turning. Even little steps in the right direction, like clearing a corner in her office, or finding the right workspace table, helped her get a bit closer, which was incredibly satisfying for her.

The notion that "you can't have it all" misses the point. People say it in an attempt to keep you grounded, but the underlying message we take from it is, "You can't have it all, so you should just work and not do things you enjoy."

Wrong.

Unfortunately, too many of us have forgotten the practice of play, and now we've grown and evolved and we don't remember what we enjoy. Perhaps your interests have changed, and shooting hoops like you did in high school no longer looks enticing. That's okay. Just because you liked it as a child doesn't mean you have to like it as an adult.

Simply put, now is the time to discover the things that make you the happiest, and make time to do them.

I'm an avid scrapbooker. I used to scrapbook 3–5 times a year by going to the local scrapbooking store on Friday nights from six to midnight. I like preserving memories. I like paper crafting. I like that scrapbooking is a social activity that lets me chat with friends while I do it. And I like that it provides a way to connect to others who share the same interest. As my schedule, children, and aspirations have grown, keeping up the practice has become more difficult, but any time I even consider giving it up, my heart breaks a little. Now, I only scrapbook once a year during a "scrapbook weekend." Even though it's less frequent than I would like, it's something I plan and look forward to every year. It rejuvenates me and connects me to what's important in so many ways.

What rejuvenates you? What activities restore you to your complete self?

THE LIFE BALANCE MYTH

I don't like the term "life balance." I believe it's a myth, and the more you chase it, the more it eludes you.

After the birth of my second child, I struggled getting back into the swing of my demanding work-at-home responsibilities. Entrepreneurs don't get maternity leave, and on top of that, Seth Godin was speaking at our biggest Startup Princess event just six weeks after I delivered. It was a crazy time.

I started looking at my other entrepreneur friends and saying to myself, "She has five kids. What does she know that I don't?" or "How does she make it look so easy?" I shared some of these questions with a friend and she responded, "Honey, you'll get there. You just need a little life balance."

The term wasn't new to me, but I had never studied it, so I set out to learn more about this magical solution. I read books and online articles, asked friends how they found life balance, and I prayed. The more I worried about it, the less fulfilled I felt. I couldn't help but think there was some secret I was missing that everyone else knew.

This went on for about nine months. While on my quest, Danielle LaPorte came to speak at the fall Startup Princess Conference in Salt Lake City. She's a mother also, so I sought her advice. I asked her how she felt about life balance, and what she does to juggle entrepreneurship and motherhood. I don't remember her exact response, but it was something like, "Life balance doesn't exist. It's about priorities." Our conversation was cut short as she got pulled away, but something clicked for me in that instant, and everything fell into place. As a planner and productivity junkie, I understood priorities, so what she said resonated with me.

That moment was a turning point for me. I revamped my life and my schedule, and things started to work again. I created my own time-management system and a roles-and-goals activity that helped me get centered on my roles as a mother, wife, friend, business owner, daughter, and so forth. I also changed the way I approached my business and my personal time. After I ironed out a few wrinkles, my consulting and coaching practices changed and I began to share the systems and mindset I created to help others realize they don't have to choose between a thriving career and a meaningful personal life. It has nothing to do with balance. With some insightful prioritization you can have both.

Life balance is a myth. Here's why:

1. Balance assumes that things are even, so life balance means you have an even distribution of time in each role you play. When I picture Lady Justice holding her scale, I think of there being the same weight on each side so it's even. If you work full-time outside the home, let's say you're gone for nine hours, is it even possible for you to spend nine hours with family and friends each day? Nope. Under that scenario, you'll never be able to spend the same amount of time in your social ventures and personal relationships as you do at the office. See, even talking about it this way is depressing.
2. If we obsess about staying balanced, then we start to keep tabs on things that depress us. We start to focus on a ticking clock, which adds one more stress to our lives. If we accept that we can never be fully in balance, we release that stress (and dare I say, guilt) and focus on spending our time doing what we most want. For example, I spend less time with my husband than I do with my children, because I'm home with my children all day. That

doesn't mean I love my husband any less. I spend less time on spiritual and religious studies and worship than I do on work. That doesn't mean my relationship with Deity is less important than my job. When we look at it from this perspective, we start to see it's not about the amount of time, but rather about how those roles are prioritized and how we spend our time when we're in those roles that makes the difference.

3. Life balance inaccurately assumes that achieving it is the only path to happiness and bliss. All the articles and books out there that suggest life balance is possible only add to the feeling that you're showing up a day late and dollar short and that you've got some catching up to do. That kind of energy around who you are and where you spend your time isn't necessary. You can be incredibly out of balance, and blissfully happy, so don't wait for the stars to align to feel happiness now, and don't buy into the lie that you have to wait to have it.
4. The life balance fallacy implies there's a secret. The real secret is this—there is no specific blueprint or system that, if you only knew what it was, could take you instantly to a peaceful state. Personal development and self-mastery cannot begin from a sense of inadequacy. Though we all feel that way to a certain extent, happiness and success are derived first from a foundation of gratitude and presence. The thought that you can't be happy until everything is "right" is a lie. I have never once been able to say, "Finally, my life is perfect!" I'm a work-in-progress, and no book, seminar, or podcast has all the answers. You just need to find what works for you.

Since balance isn't achievable, and prioritization is, remember that life changes. One week I'll have a big event at work, and the next will be slower, giving me more time to spend with my kids and do things on my wish play list. Then it swaps again the next week. We have to be flexible enough to change with our shifting schedules and priorities.

That being said, beware that in your flexible prioritized state you don't give up on the regular high performance practices that keep you in check and on the road to where you need to be. You can always move block times to accommodate the greatest need, but don't delete important blocks that keep you healthy and energized, keep your business pipeline flowing, and keep your relationships humming.

My cousin Joe is a high performer who understands the importance of play. He runs multiple companies—I know about three of them, and I'm sure there are more. What I love about Joe is that he knows what it takes to invest in his career, but he also knows how to play with the best of them. He sometimes works into the wee hours of the morning, but then he takes four or five big trips a year. He loves to travel, a bug we both inherited from our travel agent grandfather, and heads to at least one new place yearly, while also making time for old favorites like boating on Lake Powell in Utah.

There's no fast track to success. High performers work. They put into practice the principles found in this book day in and day out. Luckily, one of those principles is to master the art of play.

What does play look like for you?

Do you like to travel, or are you more athletic and sporty? Do you like to craft and create, or are you more interested in politics and current events? Do you like to stay home and curl up with a good book, or are you more outdoorsy? Are you all of the above? There are no right or wrong ways to play. It's all about what makes you happy.

Take some time to make a "Play List" of things you enjoy doing for fun. In fact, I would suggest you create two Play Lists, with at least 25 things on each. One should be your Free Play List for free and easily accessible things and activities (i.e. reading a book, watching a movie, playing a sport with friends, taking a hike, soaking in the hot tub, crafting, etc.). I use this list for quick rewards for a job well done, or as my go-to resource when I've had a rough day and need a recharge. The other is your Wish Play List for more expensive, higher reward activities (i.e. dream travel, massages, pedicures, hotel stays in your hometown, etc.). These activities are part of what drives me to perform financially.

Both lists can be motivating and useful in different ways. Thinking about the future is very valuable for high performers. We like to have something fun to work toward. Earning is part of the accomplishment. Even dates on the calendar help us keep our heads down when it's time to work, and play hard when it's time to relax. Once I know what's on my Wish Play List, it goes on my vision board and in my Ideal LifeVision so I can put my brain to work on how it might manifest itself into my life. Taking a break to do something on my Free Play List helps me relieve a little stress so I can get back to work and continue giving my best effort.

All work and no play makes you a workaholic. Figuring out the time and place for work and play, and honoring both, will bring you more joy and fulfillment than any paycheck or place you live. We could all use a little more play to remind ourselves why we work. Work to live, and play to live.

I picked "savor" as my word of the year in 2014. With a full calendar and lots of things on my Family Play List, I wanted to make sure I enjoyed the moments as they came. I wanted to enjoy the time my kids were at home, and I wanted to create happy memories with them doing simple things in our own backyard. I wanted to have opportunities to smile at them more and to just sit and chat. I wanted to enjoy the people I met and savor our time together. I didn't want to rush from place to place and not experience the minutes I was given.

High performers create moments worth savoring. They create jobs they love and a lifestyle worth fighting for to Make It Happen.

PLAY IN ACTION

- Schedule some time in the next week to write at least 25 things on your Free Play List. You're welcome to add and subtract things over time, but you'll want to start generating a healthy list.
- Schedule some time in the next week to write at least 25 things on your Wish Play List. If 25 things don't immediately come to mind, this list can be a work in progress, too.
- If you have been neglecting the play in your high performance lifestyle, I want you to do one item on your Free Play List each day. It doesn't have to be a huge time commitment each day, but get back into playing so you can remember what you do and don't like.
- Where appropriate, find images that represent the items on your Wish Play List. Put them on your vision board. I recommend putting no more than seven items at a time from your Wish Play List on your vision board, so start with the ones you want the soonest. Don't worry—with the life you have ahead of you, you'll get more done. We just have to focus our efforts to get things rolling. If you need more explanation on this, revisit the chapter POSSIBILITY.
- If you have stored up a bunch of vacation days, I want you to start to use them. Take one day off in the next three weeks so you can have a whole day of play (and while you're at it, you can work in a little planning session, too! Ahem, I think my play may have just oozed in here.)
- If you're a stay-at-home mom thinking, "Nice thought, but moms don't get vacation days," take heart. You still need a little play in your life, and there are ways to work some of your Free Play List into your day. Always keep a book going, put a warm bath in your Power Down routine, craft, create, or do

something that feels like a vacation at home. Schedule some time away, too. If you have a supportive spouse, find a time you can get away on a regular basis. If your circumstances don't allow for that, trade "time off" with a friend. Watch her kids while she takes a break, and have her watch your kids while you take a break.

- Some of your Play List items might need some chunking down. Take some time to break down big goals into small, simple things you can do to move forward. Remember the advice I gave my client from the beginning of the chapter? If you want a craft room for creating, write down the action items needed to Make It Happen. Sometimes taking little steps can be incredibly fulfilling, and it gets you that much closer to the dream.
- Every now and again, put new things on your Play Lists. Learn a new language or instrument, try a new athletic activity, read a book outside your favorite genre. Part of high performance and being a well-rounded individual comes from branching out. You don't have to love all the new things you try, but at least you can say you tried them (and you'll be better off for it, too!)

CHAPTER 18

A PATTERN FOR RAISING UP LITTLE HIGH PERFORMERS

"All kids need is a little help, a little hope and somebody who believes in them."

—Magic Johnson

People often come up to me after hearing the keynote version of this book and ask, "How can I help my kids get this information now, so they don't have to wait until they're 30 or 40 to have the tools for success?"

Wouldn't it be wonderful if we lived in a world where all adults, regardless of whether they had kids of their own, shared the responsibility to raise up high performers? How would our society and economy change if the generations after us were driven, positive, and success-minded?

Before I continue, I can't help but mention that no goal, no amount of preparation, and no tradition will do more to help raise good kids than huge doses of love and presence. It's a good reminder to us all, myself included, that you can try to force goals on kids, but if they don't know they are loved, high performance won't matter or be a priority for them. If nothing else, show an abundance of love to all the kids in your life. Be present when you're with them by putting away your phone and technology. Listen. Share. Keep your commitments.

I'm no parenting expert; my children are young and I still have a lot to learn about raising them. That being said, I've had the opportunity to evaluate my childhood, and chat with friends about how to raise good kids. I've certainly tried some things that have failed, but I have found some effective practices that everyone can implement as we take on the important responsibility of building up the world's youth.

I call these practices "anchor points." In nautical terms, anchors are used to connect boats and vessels of any size with the land beneath a body of water. Anchors provide stability and keep vessels from moving with the wind or current. Similarly, these practices will help our youth find stability by anchoring them to the things that matter most. In the midst of the storms of life and winds of the world, these practices provide a much needed foundation that children and teenagers crave in their lives.

If you picture a boat anchor, you'll realize that each one typically has a minimum of two stabilizing points. For the anchor to be effective, at least one of these points must be positioned correctly and make a deep connection to land. Each of the following suggestions is effective in teaching the practices of high performance. Some may be more suited than others to connect with your children, or the children in your life. Hopefully, as you try several anchor points, at least one of them will stick.

POSITIVITY

As a parent, a teacher, or an influencer, changing the future starts with *you* being a happy and positive person. Nobody likes a "Debbie Downer," and children pick up on negative tones and attitudes, even when they aren't directed at them. Avoid conversations at the dinner table and around little ears about your distaste for current politicians, or the frustrations of empty pocketbooks. Watch what you say about how much you hate your work, or the problems you're having with the neighbors. I don't discredit the very real frustrations of these issues, but consider the consequences of all the negative talk around impressionable children and teenagers. Do you want them to be doom and gloom all the time? Do you want them looking for the worst in others or themselves? Create conversations that are inspiring and uplifting and help kids look for the good around them.

Though some might argue we're not doing kids any favors by giving them rose- colored glasses, I say negativity abounds. Children look to parents and influencers to see how *we* respond to these circumstances. You can share facts and you can share truth, but you can also powerfully share the fact that despite the challenges of life, happiness and positive thinking are great ways to weather the storms. Love life, and your kids will want to do the same.

If you want your kids to be happy, successful, and performance-driven adults, teach them how to respond so they can find joy in the everyday. Ask them at the end of the day, "What was the best thing that happened to you today?" Create a practice around acknowledging the good. This question works well at the dinner table or when you're tucking them into bed at night. At the beginning they may have a hard time pinpointing something, but as time goes by they'll be trained to look for the good throughout day, and will often beat you to the question when they have great things to share.

Don't forget to share your wins from the day, too. Let them see you putting positivity in action.

If you're going for a gold medal in raising high performers (and I hope you are), ask a powerful follow up question, "What did you do to *make* someone else happy today?" This helps them become more aware of others. Start now to instill in your children that they have the ability to influence the happiness of others. Teaching them to be service-minded will also make huge deposits in their own success bank.

When children approach you with negative commentary, help them reframe their thoughts. Use this approach with negative body image and self-esteem issues as well. In time kids will do it for themselves and will naturally look on the positive side of life.

Having a special family word, phrase, or activity will help provide an anchor point to remind your kids to reframe and practice positivity. This could be as simple as saying "reframe" or some other trigger word to help them get back on a positive note, or it could be a more interactive activity. I took a class where the teacher required us to say ten positive things about ourselves (or others) for every negative thing we verbalized. This not only helped eliminate negative talk and stress the importance of speaking positively, but it also gave an opportunity to seek the positive. Kids will find great things about themselves and others if they are encouraged to look for them.

Finally, help children choose happiness. I remember sitting down with my very young children and talking about how happiness is a choice. Now when they are being ornery, talking back, or are upset about something I said "No" to, I simply say, "Choose to be happy." It helps remind them that negativity is a choice.

GRATITUDE

Take it one step further and help your kids express gratitude for their blessings on a regular basis. Ask them to tell you two things for which they are grateful. Help them find a simple notebook to keep every night. If your kids are too little to write (like mine are) have them draw pictures of the things they appreciate.

My children are growing up with more than I had when I was their age. Though I have a great deal of gratitude for our current circumstances, I want my children to know and understand that other kids don't have the same things. I don't want them to take for granted the things they think are normal. We have real conversations about kids who don't have beds, or heat, or even a home. We ask our kids every night for two things they are thankful for. They express them to us, and also express them in their prayers. It's been a huge blessing for my kids.

On a humorous side note, my husband told my kids about cultures and history where the bathrooms are outside and people had to bundle up in the winter to go use an outhouse that didn't flush. Of all the things we've told our kids, this one seems to have had the most staying power. My son thanks God in his prayers every night for an indoor toilet!

THINKING ABOUT THE FUTURE

Kids thrive and grow when they have opportunities to practice thinking about the future. Having something fun to look forward to helps them work through current problems or challenges with the drive to endure them.

Calendar and Discuss Future Events

Have fun things on the calendar. It can be a family vacation or a trip to the zoo or to get an ice cream cone. Write it on the calendar and talk about it to build excitement as the date approaches. I know that I love having something fun to look forward to, and I have found my kids love it, too.

One day, while dropping off my then 5-year-old son at school, he jumped out of the car and said, "Bye mom, have a good day! I look forward to having fun with you at Disneyland!" I had told the kids that morning that we were going to go see "the mouse" soon, and we had enjoyed talking about the rides we wanted to go on and the food we wanted to eat. I thought it was interesting how a few hours later that's what he thought about as he was on his way to school.

Turns out, he's just as excited when we plan a trip to the city pool or the park. Giving kids a reason to hang on when reality feels a little rough doesn't have to cost a lot of money.

Involve Them in Planning Fun Things

As one mom I know was contemplating the approaching unstructured summer vacation, she wondered how many times she would hear her kids complain about being bored, or worse, how often she would have to pull them away from the TV. This seems to be a reality for most moms, even when kids are surrounded by toys and activities. As a preemptive strike, she sat down with her kids at the beginning of summer break, pulled out some local magazines, and together they built a summer vision board. They cut out pictures of a nearby national park they wanted to visit. They used pictures of mountains to represent hikes they wanted to go on. They talked about which swimming pools they wanted to hit, and figured out some times they could have friends over for easy back yard water parties. They discussed the number of pages they could read during the summer, and they built a challenge around reading. It was a bonding time just creating the board, and it was even more fun keeping track of the dates on the back of the board as they completed activities throughout the summer.

This isn't about becoming big party planners for your kids. Sometimes the best thing we can do is tell them to find something on their own. This gets them using their imaginations and not depending on us to create activities for them. This is much easier if they have a great list to pull from. Then you can say, "Check the fun board!" and again, they're thinking about the future. Even if every day isn't a party, they'll know fun times are in store.

"Imagine If"

I started a little activity with my kids when they were just two and four. After we finish the nightly routine and they are tucked in bed, I turn off the light and lie down on the floor. Then I ask some simple, "Imagine if…" questions and they take turns answering. The goal is to get them thinking, dreaming, and wishing for the future.

Here are some of our favorites:

- Imagine if we went Disneyland, what ride would you like to go on first?
- Imagine if we went to the park, what friends would you like to have there with you?
- Imagine if you could buy a new bike or toy, what would choose?
- Imagine if you could have any kind of treat tomorrow, what would you pick?
- Imagine if we could paint your room any color, what color would you want it?
- Imagine if we went to see grandma, what would you want to tell her?

Sometimes these chats turn into memory sessions where my kids remind me of things that happened on family trips. Awesome! Sometimes, these questions lead into great conversations about how to earn trips or fun toys they want. Even better! Never once have they insisted we do something just because we talked about it in "Imagine if…"

We don't do "Imagine if…" every night. It's something special we only do from time to time, but they are happy times with just me and my kids. I'm helping them form the beginning of goals and fostering in them thoughts of dreaming big!

This also might be a fun activity to do in the car. If you feel the only time you have with your kids is shuttling them from school to activities, use that time to connect. "Imagine if…," gratitude-listing, and other anchor points are great car conversations!

TRADITIONS

In an unstable world, our youth crave comfort. Comfort can come through having basic needs met—food, clothing, shelter, water, and ultimately a lot of love. I've found traditions are a great way to show love and comfort. Even during difficult times in my childhood, I often thought of fun memories of the past and felt the joy and hope that they would happen again.

There are some obvious traditions around birthdays and holidays that bring great joy. Keep doing those, but what else can you put in place to provide some simple, yet profound experiences for the kids in your life?

As I was growing up with a single mom, Valentine's Day was a fun family holiday. My parents weren't off on dates so my mom would cook a meal and place a little unwrapped prize under our plates. We couldn't flip the plates over until after the prayer on the meal. It was a fun, simple tradition that I looked forward to. So much so that I do the same with my kids now, and my husband and I go out on a different day. After all, who wants to brave the restaurant wait times and clamor for a sitter on a day like that?

Good family friends of ours have a Friday night pizza tradition. Sarah, the mom, makes the pizza from scratch (and has perfected the recipe over the years), and Friday is a fun family food/movie/game playing night. It's something the kids look forward to and talk about all week. Other families I know have Taco Tuesday, or Spaghetti Wednesday, or Dad cooks Saturday breakfast and eats with the kids (the kids *and* mom benefit there). What traditions could you institute around meals or regular activities?

We have what we call "Family Home Evening" at our house every Monday night. We use this time to teach an important spiritual or value-based principle, chat with our kids, have a fun activity and treat, and spend time together without cell phones or technology. We also "synchronize our calendars" during this time and make sure we have everyone's events documented so we can cheer on big tests, tournaments, or projects coming up for the week. This is absolutely free, and our kids ask for it every night. What benefits could you and your family gain from a night unplugged, or a family game night, or a values night? It's powerful for comfort and connection.

On a side note, my mother had Family Home Evening with us regularly. We took turns "conducting" the meeting and giving the short lessons. Though simple, these experiences gave us opportunities to present and perform in a comfortable space. Today, all four of her children enjoy speaking and presenting. Through those experiences, we got practice and encouragement. Can you see a simple yet significant secondary benefit and power of simple traditions to raising up high performers?

I love the principle that by small and simple things great things can come to fruition. Traditions help kids define themselves and find comfort in relationships.

If you don't have the benefit of having your children or even kids you want to influence in your home, take heart. There are many co-parenting families and adults without children of their own who are able to influence nieces, nephews, neighbors, and friends.

How about a monthly ice cream trip? Something they can look forward to, but doesn't cost a lot. It's the routine and the practice that makes it special. You could even make a theme out of it. Perhaps you want to find the best soft serve ice cream in the city, so for one year you try twelve places, and vote for your favorite.

I admit that traditions around food are my favorite, but there are so many other options. This can also be done with finding a favorite park, hike, walking tour, bike ride, etc. What traditions can you create around the kids you love that will help them foster their talents in sports or the arts? Monthly play dates? Movie nights? Soccer games? Karaoke singing?

You get the idea. Now go, think of some traditions you can implement with the youth closest to you.

ANNUAL THEMES: FAMILY

Stephen Covey encouraged families everywhere to come up with a mission statement. He talked about the importance of sitting down together, talking about priorities, and writing a statement to anchor the family in values and behavior. I like mission statements and think they are a great addition to a positive and thriving family culture. Mission statements are enduring and probably don't change much over time. For that reason, I like the idea of also having themes—shorter statements, sentences, or even single words that change as your kids develop and grow.

A theme is a goal or value in a simple statement. As you consider themes for and with your kids, keep these three things in mind.

Themes should be simple and age appropriate. Don't create long family themes, even as kids grow up. Simple themes make bigger impressions. Different from family mission statements that may appropriately be lengthier, a theme should be a focus for a set period of time, ideally about a year.

Themes should be memorable. Each person in your family should be able to memorize it in one sitting. If you want them to be able to repeat it at any given moment, keep it snappy.

Themes should be actionable. The idea is to create something that ignites change and will come to their mind at key moments. If you decide to incorporate Family Home Evenings into your family's high performance practices, these themes can be discussed during those gatherings. Talk together. Share ideas as to how they can take action, and let them share ideas and think through scenarios as well.

Let's look at a couple of examples of family themes to get your brain thinking.

The Jones family introduced me to short-term family themes. Their themes are timed with the school year, but you could easily institute them into the calendar year as well. One year, their theme was "Work Hard. Play Hard." Simple, memorable, and actionable. They helped their kids understand the importance of working hard in school, and also spent a lot of time playing as a family and enjoying time together.

When I asked the Jones family if I could share their story and theme, they were quick to credit family and lifestyle blogger Stephanie Nielson with the idea. Stephanie kicks off the family's annual theme with a fun dinner. The table is decorated to the nines and the kids get crowns with their names on them. I love it!

I decided to have our first family theme when our oldest started kindergarten. I thought a lot about it, and talked through ideas with my husband. In the end, we went with "Be Brave. Be Smart. Be Kind." It was perfect for my kids and their ages at the time (five and three). It was simple, they remembered it easily, and we talked about how to act on those words. We shared the theme with our kids a few days before school started, and talked about times they might need to be brave. We discussed how it's okay to be smart, and that above all, being kind to other kids is really important. The first day I dropped my son off at school, he hopped out of the car and to himself, under his breath but loud enough for me to hear, he said, "Be brave. Be smart. Be kind." I wanted to cry happy tears right then and there. He was using our theme to help him overcome his first-day jitters. That year it came up in so many ways. Situations would arise and he would come home and tell us when he applied one of the principles. It's amazing to me how simple and how powerful those six words have been.

I'm careful not to shove the theme down the kid's throats on a regular basis, but it's there as a foundation for conversations where appropriate. What's more, we're in this together, so I'm able to tell my kids about times I've had to be brave with work, or kind to someone who was mean. It helps me, too!

If you like the idea of family themes, and want to explore them even more, consider a simple tracking system to record times when your kids exhibited the theme. Perhaps you could keep a white board somewhere in your home where people can note when they put the family theme to work in their own life. Maybe there's a large jar in the kitchen where you and your kids can put written experiences when you acted on the theme. At the end of each month, you can read them aloud and celebrate the wins together!

Family themes are a way to get your kids to focus efforts and lay the groundwork for individual goals. Themes give kids a way to get their feet wet in personal development while working with other family members to achieve those goals together. It also helps them celebrate each other and work together for a common good.

Family themes can also be a good way to direct individuals who are resistant to, or have a hard time coming up with, individual goals. It provides a safe way to track.

INDIVIDUAL THEMES/GOALS

It goes without saying that having individual goals or themes can be very valuable in helping with varying personalities and interests. While family themes are broad and motivationally based, individual themes and goals are specific to a child's needs and areas of focus at the time.

My friend, Nicole Carpenter, uses the Doran/McCullough "SMARTY" Goals approach with her kids. (If you want to reference the SMARTY Goals approach, you can find it in the chapter on PLANNING.) She has them write down a goal and they use the SMARTY framework to make sure it sticks.

Some goals may be for a year, and some may be for a season that correlates with sports or lessons of some kind. What's important is how you help your kids craft a goal or destination that helps them identify progress and growth. When it's been decided, have them write it down, and then place it where they can see and refer to it often.

As I was writing this chapter, my friend Stacy shared a picture on social media showing an etching she made for her basketball-loving son, Ashton. It reads:

"Every possession, every play
every time, every way
Try your hardest…
even when it seems the darkest."

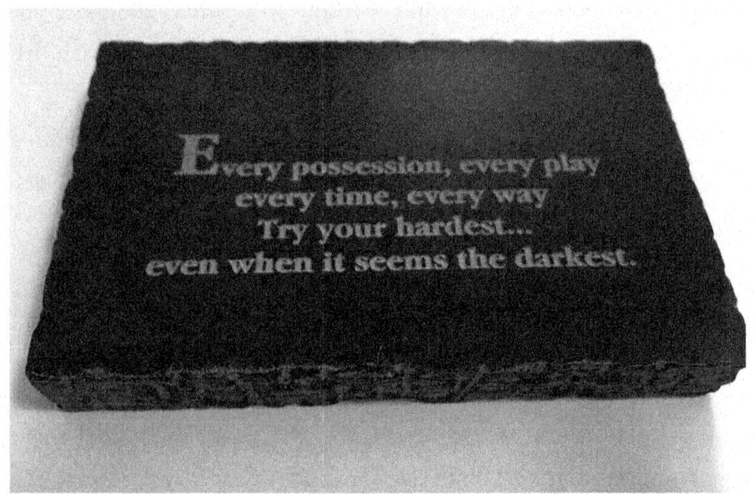

As you can imagine, I loved it, and asked how it came about for her and her son. This is what she told me:

> That little saying is all Ashton. He even has an entire rap that he wrote to help motivate himself. He is a classic perfectionist: Very particular, extremely passionate and fiercely loyal… Because he is a perfectionist, he also can get easily discouraged and intensely upset when things don't go as planned. In his highly emotional state he would not be very receptive of any "pep talks" from me, but would always come around in his own time. That is why I wanted the etching made and the contract he wrote for himself signed on his wall, for him to remind himself why he wants to succeed and why he loves what he does in the first place. He's very much like his dad in a lot of ways and me in others so I felt like I had some insight to his personality and what worked for him.

Smart kid, and an even smarter mom! I love that Stacy was aware of her son's personality and tendencies. I love that Ashton came up with something on his own (at the age of nine) that would help motivate him, and I LOVE that his parents channeled that into an anchor point he could always refer to, find comfort in, and ultimately be motivated by.

I bet he remembers this forever, just like I remember Elaine Millet and my mom telling me, "Make It Happen, Michelle!" after all these years.

GOAL PARTIES

My friend Kate grew up in a family with 10 kids. Her mom knew the value of setting goals and at the beginning of each school year the kids would each write down five personal goals.

One goal was educational—i.e. the G.P.A. they were striving to earn or the score needed on the ACT/SAT.

One goal was about relationships—i.e. making 5 new friends or not talking back to mom and dad.

One goal involved health—i.e. eating fruits and veggies every day or exercising a certain amount a week.

One goal involved something spiritual—i.e. reading scripture every day, sharing testimony with friends or consistent personal morning and evening prayers.

One goal was personal—i.e. a sport or talent they wanted to learn and cultivate.

At the end of the school year, all ten kids (and mom and dad, who also participated—what a great example!) sat around the table. They would share their goals and if/how they achieved them. When they did, everyone would cheer and mom would slide a candy bar across the table (a luxury to them). If the kids didn't reach their goals, everyone would "boo." When I heard that last part, I laughed out loud! While I probably wouldn't implement the "boo" practice in my home, I WILL say that if Kate is any indication, those 10 kids have thick skins and a strong sense of self. When we celebrate our successes and acknowledge our areas of improvement, and build a support system to grow THAT is when the magic happens.

I love the quote by Clayton Christensen, "Self-esteem comes from achieving something important when it's hard to do." If we can teach our children how to set and achieve worthy goals, we're setting them up with a foundation of confidence and giving them tools to face future.

Don't get overwhelmed. I'm not trying to say you need a family theme, *and* a family activity vision board, *and* individual themes *and* vision boards *and* goal parties.

These ideas are designed to be a jumping off point. Select the two or three practices you want to put in place with the kids in your life, or use them to springboard to even better ideas that come to you as parents and influencers. You know the kids in your life better than I do; you'll be able to find ways to connect with and motivate them.

Here are a few questions you can ask to come up with ideas unique to your youth:

How can I help the kids in my life be more positive?

What activities, games, and questions can I ask to help them be more mindful about the future?

What themes or phrases would be good to focus on in the coming year?

What are the individual goals and needs for my kids? How can I help them progress toward what THEY want most?

Above all, remember that being an example of high performance is more important than pushing it on them. Have a vision, share it with your kids, and let them watch you tackle it. Let them see how you get back on course when you may have veered a little. Show them how to stick to it when times get tough. Show them they can do hard things.

Happiness, motivation, and high performance carry with them a powerful ripple effect. When you live your best life, your kids will want to Make It Happen, too.

RAISING HIGH PERFORMERS IN ACTION

- If you feel like the only time you have with your kids is shuttling them from school to activities, use that time to connect! "Imagine if…," gratitude-listing, and other anchor points are great car conversations.
- Brainstorm some simple traditions that you can institute in your home and your routines based on your unique circumstances and needs.
- Print off some of your favorite motivational quotes and place them in your home.

- Print off and display your kids' own goals, pep talks, and keywords. Where appropriate, get vinyl lettering to put on walls, have them etched into stone, or have a designer of fivrr.com make it nice and pretty! Put them in their bedrooms and bathrooms where they can be reminded about high performance.
- Go to a discount or dollar store and buy some fun notebooks to give your kids. Talk about gratitude and have them keep the notebooks by their bed or in an easily accessible basket. Pull them out regularly and have them write or draw their blessings. These notebooks will be fun keepsakes!
- Try a goal party! What other incentives could you use? How could you remind your kids during the year to keep up on their goals with love and encouragement?

CHAPTER 19
THE PLASTIC BAG PRINCIPLE

"It's not what happens to you that defines you.
It's how you rise above."
—Michelle McCullough

I was only seven at the time, but the memory of that night is still clear as ever.

It was past my bedtime. I was playing in my room, trying to go undetected, and thinking I was somehow cheating the system. When my mom finally came into my room, she handed me a plastic grocery sack and told me, "Pack some clothes. We're going to Grandma's house and I don't know when we're coming back."

I can't recall if I asked a lot of questions, but I distinctly remember putting a few items of clothing in my bag, and then adding some of my seven-year-old treasures—toys and all the coins to my name (which was probably less than fifty cents). The heavier items sank to the bottom of the bag and pulled it downward, and I carefully carried it as we walked past my dad, who sat crying on the stairs. In my mind I can still see his figure illuminated through the window as we drove away in the dark.

Isn't it interesting the things we remember (and the things we forget) years later? I've never looked at that event as being overly traumatic, and it has never caused the need for any professional counseling sessions. However, the experience has given me a good mental image for the baggage we all carry.

I'll bet if you and I were to sit down, you could tell me some crazy and maybe even downright depressing situations you've encountered in your life. If we invited a few neighbors or friends, there's no doubt they could each tell us stories that would make us cringe or cry.

Each of us has baggage in some form or another. Some is more public than others. Some is more tragic than others. But no matter what, we all have something. Divorce, abuse, loss of a loved one, loss of a job, severe economic consequences, significant health issues, caring for an ailing spouse or parent, caring for a child with disabilities—the list goes on and on.

It's easy to get caught up comparing hardships and trying to outdo one another in a "my life is worse than yours" kind of competition. At times I have to remind myself of the old saying, "If problems were clothing all hung on the line, you'd take yours, and I'd take mine." Life is hard in its own way for each of us, but it's not your past or circumstances that define you.

When my mother handed me that grocery sack, I could have asked her a lot of questions. I could have requested a nicer bag. After all, my grandfather was a travel agent and we had Pan AM overnight bags in abundance in our house. But in the midst of her own trial (arguably more traumatic than mine) she needed a quick solution for an unplanned event. Besides, what difference would it have made? We can package our trials however we want, but they still remain the same. They are still trials, and we can choose to dwell on them or deal with them. We can look at them as something temporary we will carry with us for a time before leaving them behind, or we can make them a permanent fixture in our lives that we lug with us into every relationship, employment opportunity, and circumstance.

Don't spend your whole life wishing your "bag" was different. You have to use what you've got, learn from the experiences, and move on to create a better future.

Again, I know many people will say, "Your parents got divorced when you were seven? That isn't nearly as traumatic as ______________________." I get it. I could tell you some of my other life events and hardships to try and convince you I've been through trials, but the same principle would apply. It's not a competition, it's an experience. Don't let your bag become your identity, or an excuse to "one-up" others in conversation.

I was at a live event when I first heard the story of Sam Bracken. His childhood was fraught with trial and drama. He was abused by his step-father and started using drugs and alcohol by the age of nine. He struggled through school, but with the help of caring teachers and his involvement in sports, he was able to turn his life around. Then, just as things were looking up, his mother abandoned him when he was fifteen, and he was left homeless with only the clothes on his back and a few other possessions in an orange sports duffle bag.

As I listened to Bracken, who later became a scholar, star athlete, and successful business executive, I was moved. Then he taught a powerful life principle. He said, "Fill your bag with hopes and dreams instead of fear and insecurities."

Dwelling on what's not right will *never* bring you the success and happiness you desire. Choosing success despite your challenges will give you power and purpose beyond measure. However, if you've spent most of your life dwelling in the past or wallowing in self-pity, it may take a while to retrain your brain (and even your relationships) to a point that you're willing to make that kind of shift. Again, remember it takes practice. If you're finding it hard to simply move on, you may want to consider seeking professional help to get you on your way.

One of the most powerful practices of high performers is to overcome the past and become something better. They don't let their circumstances, past or current, keep them from high achievement. They acknowledge the experiences for what they are— stepping stones. You have that choice, too. Each trial in your life is designed to teach you something and move you further down the path of progression. When you look at them from that standpoint, you can face and overcome them in powerful ways.

Whether you're seven or seventy-seven, it's not too late to accept what's in your bag and make the most of it. The principles and practices in this book are designed to help you do just that, so as a final note in practicing high performance, I encourage you to embrace your past and your present so you can choose the future you really want.

I've provided a lot of ideas, tools and resources to help you practice high performance. Now it's up to you to Make It Happen!

THE PLASTIC BAG PRINCIPLE IN ACTION

- If I haven't convinced you already, I'll mention it again: start your own gratitude journal and write down five things you're grateful for every day. Just try it.
- Take "The Challenge, Challenge": Get out a piece of paper. Write a current or past challenge at the top. (If you want, you can name it something like, "My Amazing Divorce" or "My Growth Cancer Experience" to put a positive spin. If it's too fresh, just the challenge at the top will do. ;) Then list 10 things

that that particular adversity or trial has taught you. When we look on the bright side of our baggage, it's easier to work through it. Keep these in a book for reference, if you wish.

- Try the "Control, No Control" exercise. (This exercise is great if you're currently in the middle of the challenge and you want to work through it a little better.) Take a piece of paper. Fold it in half or draw a line down the middle. On one side write "Control" on the other side write "No Control". Think about the circumstances you're in, if there are items you can control write them down in the "control column." The items/circumstances you can't control go in the "no control column." Once they are documented, focus on the actions you CAN take and don't worry about the ones you can't.
- Teach someone else about the Plastic Bag Principle. Do your kids need this? Spouse? Friend? Ask if it would be okay for you to tell them a story and help them see their baggage through a different light.

ACKNOWLEDGMENTS

Many thanks to my editor Melanie Donahoo, who is a miracle worker. Melanie, you have a literary gift. I will always have a little twinge of jealousy about it. More than anything else, I'm just grateful for your friendship. I'm lucky to have you on both sides of my personal and professional fence. (Perhaps I should have let you edit my acknowledgments chapter, too.)

Also, thanks to Denae Handy, London Schade, Rachel Ramsay, and Micah Page for the editing, layout, and production of the first version of this book when I self-published. Thanks to Evelyn Jeffries for the final copyediting. Thanks also to SplitSeed for formatting.

To my mom, my friends, and my husband, I couldn't have done this without you. This book is a mix of every speaking engagement, live event, and consulting client where you supported me and had my kids. I bow to you.

Thanks to all the folks at Morgan James Publishing, and especially for David Hancock, who allowed a girl to have a dream—and then made it come true. When I attended Brendon Burchard's Experts Academy in September of 2011, David Hancock was there. Experts from all over the country and throughout the world pitched their books to David. At the time, this book was just a dream, and I didn't know if it would ever happen, but I stood in line anyway. When I got up there I said, "I don't have anything to pitch you yet, but I'd like a picture of the two of us holding a pretend book that I could put on my vision board. He humored me—and I'm so glad he did. Now there will be pictures of the two of us holding the finished product. Make It Happen in ACTION!

To my Heavenly Father, this project reconfirmed to me your existence and that you know who I am. When I first decided to write this book, I wrote more than 20,000 words in ten days. Miraculous. I am forever grateful. Although it took me two years to complete the second edition, it was as it should be. You taught me things through that process I couldn't have learned any other way. All I am I give to you. All the shortcomings herein are mine.

CONTACT MICHELLE

I would love to connect with you! I welcome your comments and questions!

inquiry@speakmichelle.com

Website: http://www.speakmichelle.com

Facebook: http://www.facebook.com/speakmichelle

Make It Happen Radio Show: http://www.michelleontheair.com

BOOK MICHELLE TO SPEAK

If you know a group or organization that would benefit from this message at an upcoming event, please contact Michelle about speaking opportunities.

http://www.speakmichelle.com

Michelle McCullough started her first business when she was 19 and currently runs 3 companies including consulting other businesses all over the world. A seasoned speaker, Michelle teaches success principles and leadership insights that help boost employee engagement and higher performance. In addition to running her own consulting businesses, Michelle is the managing director for Startup Princess, listed by Forbes as "One of the top 10 resources for Women Entrepreneurs". She's worked with top brands like Visa Small Business, UPS Store, AWeber and more. She's spoken for the Air Force Reserve, Goldman Sachs and Ancestry.com, among others. She's been featured in entrepreneur.com, in the 40 under 40, Fox TV and has been interviewed for television and radio over 100 times, including Good Morning America and The Today Show. She was recently named in the Top 100 Small Business Influencers with Inc Magazine, Michael Gerber and Grant Cardone. Her own radio show "Make It Happen" has over 1 million downloads.

MORE FROM MICHELLE

MAKE IT HAPPEN RADIO

About the show:

You're a big thinker with plenty of vision, heart, and passion.

You've got a big idea, a business you want to build, and/or a dream you're ready to achieve.

So how do you bring that vision into reality?

How do you unlock the step by step plan to the Big Picture of YOU—your life, your business, and your success?

Enter Michelle McCullough.

Successful serial entrepreneur, acclaimed speaker, and *The Woohoo Radio Network*'s resident Business and Success Strategist. Michelle has used her marketing know-how to help countless business owners achieve their goals by implementing proven, strategic methods, and she has the smarts, strategies, and experience to help you improve your life and take your business to the next level.

Whether you're struggling to balance your business and personal life, wondering how to get more customers through the door, looking for ways to work smarter, or are overwhelmed by the everyday stresses of being a business owner, Michelle can help.

Listen on iTunes: http://www.bit.ly/MIHRiTunes

Check out past episodes and learn more about the show at http://www.michelleontheair.com

THE LIVING ROOM

About the show:

Do you ever wonder if you're the only woman who runs errands in yoga pants so it will look like she went to the gym? Or how about the only mom who feeds her kids raw cookie dough? Or do you think you're the only one who "cooks" her family cereal for dinner?

Do you need more laughter and less loudness, more self-love and less self-loathing, more joy and less judgment?

You're not alone.

Come to The Living Room, a place where we get comfy, candid, and confident together. Come seeking sanctuary and leave feeling renewed. We're saving a seat for you! Give yourself some Living Room today.

Listen on iTunes: http://bit.ly/TLRShowiTunes

Learn more about the show, meet our co-hosts and find past episodes go to http://bit.ly/TLRShowiTunes

THE SOCIAL MEDIA BLUEPRINT

Are you ready to eliminate the mystery and overwhelm of using social media and take your business from social media clueless to social media confident? With this new Social Media Blueprint you'll learn how to master these online networks to grow your fan base and your business.

Learn more and get your copy at http://www.speakmichelle.com/socialmedia

FOR THE
DEVELOPING WORLD
LIBRARY
FOR ALL
DIGITAL LIBRARY

CPSIA information can be obtained
at www.ICGtesting.com
Printed in the USA
BVOW04s0336130517
483970BV00001BA/121/P